The HIDDEN POWER IN YOUR DNA:

How to Use Genealogy to Explore Ancestral Patterns & Transform Your Life

by

Judy Wilkins-Smith

Other books by Judy Wilkins-Smith

Decoding your Emotional Blueprint: A Powerful Guide to Transformation Through Disentangling Multigenerational Patterns [Sounds True, 2022]

> "In this brilliant book, executive coach Judy Wilkins-Smith shows how these are often unconscious patterns passed down through generations from our ancestors. She shows how a single thought or word—our 'emotional DNA'—can curb our potential. We're surrounded by systems that keep these blockages in place, and until we learn to crack the code, we reenact our family patterns. I recommend this book highly both for clinicians and as a self-help guide."
>
> **—Dawson Church, PhD, author of The Genie in Your Genes**

ISBN 979-8-218-39890-3

Text copyright © Judy Wilkins-Smith, 2024

System Dynamics

Cover design by Eric Labacz
Typography and layout by Andrea Scholz

All rights reserved.
No part of this book shall be reproduced or utilized in any form or by any means, electronic or mechanical, without prior permission in writing from Judy Wilkins-Smith.

www.judywilkins-smith.com

TABLE OF CONTENTS

Dear Reader — p. 6

Introduction — p. 9

PART I: Epigenetics, Brain Plasticity, Identifying & Understanding Ancestral Patterns — p. 17

Chapter One: A Quick Look at Epigenetics and Brain (Neuro) Plasticity — p. 19

Chapter Two: How To Know You're Entangled In a Multi-Generational Pattern — p. 33

Chapter Three: How Ancestral Patterns Affect Us — p. 45

PART II: Genealogy 2.0 — p. 67

Chapter Four: Meta-events and Meta-patterns — p. 69

Chapter Five: Linking Meta-events and Emotional DNA Patterns — p. 85

Chapter Six: Finding Meta-Data Locations — p. 105

PART III - Genealogy 3.0 — p. 111

Chapter Seven: Putting It All Together — p. 113

Chapter Eight: You Are the Game Changer — p. 129

END NOTES — p. 138

Dear Reader ~

Once upon a time we thought that knowing our genealogy linked us to our ancestors by giving us our place in our family line/system and that was that. However, it turns out that was just the beginning.

There are three distinctly different stages to genealogy, not just one. Genealogy 1.0, Genealogy 2.0, and Genealogy 3.

Each stage contains clues about who you are—not just where you come from geographically and ethnically, but how you think, feel and act in the world. The information contained in each of the three stages of genealogy builds from one stage to the next, eventually giving you tremendous personal insights into your possibilities, limitations, and potentials for success in life.

Whether you know a lot about your family history or have never even met your parents, a simple saliva sample is the doorway to all three stages of genealogy. Not only can this kind of testing show you where you come from, reveal your bloodlines and unveil your ethnic/geographic background (what I call Genealogy 1.0), if you take it a step further, in Genealogy 2.0, you can uncover emotional, physical, and psychological information about what makes you tick.

In Genealogy 3.0 you can discover hidden emotional patterns, habitual ways of thinking and acting, unconscious loyalties, and subconscious programs embedded in your DNA that affect your life in ways you would never have guessed. These inherited patterns are called Emotional DNA.

In this book you will learn how to identify those patterns and programs, and begin to learn how to change your Emotional DNA and transform your life.

So—for all you serious and not-so-serious genealogists out there, two more branches are waiting for you explore. Genealogy 1.0 was just the beginning.

Welcome to the next chapter.

Enjoy the ride!

Judy Wilkins-Smith

INTRODUCTION

Jesse's mom and dad adopted her shortly after her birth and she loved them dearly. All the same, she couldn't help wondering what her biological parents were like and where they'd come from—where she'd come from. When her friends at work got together and bought her a genealogy package (including an autosomal DNA "spit kit") for her 30th birthday, she'd been thrilled.

She learned a lot from the DNA information—her family was mostly from Eastern Europe and the Middle East, with some interesting ancestral connections in India. (Maybe that's where her interest in yoga and meditation came from!?) But there were also a lot of questions the maps and charts raised but couldn't answer.

She'd even sent the raw data to a company that analyzes SNPS. But what could single-nucleotide polymorphisms and markers for joined earlobes tell her about resolving her personal issues? *What about my anxiety disorder and bouts of depression?* she wondered. *Where do they come from? Why do I feel so restless and dissatisfied? Why do I keep changing jobs all the time? Help!*

Genealogy 1.0

Exploring your ancestry is exciting and can tell you a lot. It can give you a sense of belonging, continuity, connection and place. It can reveal history, religious ethnicity and physical predispositions for possible health issues. It can help you develop an effective workout program and find long lost third cousins in Belfast and Brazil.

This process of discovery is "normal genealogy"—what I call Genealogy 1.0.

Unfortunately, Genealogy 1.0 tells you nothing about your emotional DNA—inherited patterns of thoughts, feelings and actions that end up unconsciously running your life. It tells you nothing about your emotional issues and habits, your hot buttons and potential. It fails to reveal how you can effectively deal with these issues and resolve them in a healthy manner. It doesn't show you how to grow as a better person. It can't because it's all about your physical DNA, physical influences and physical relationships.

But Genealogy 3.0 changes all that. How? Well, before we get to that, first I have to tell you about Genealogy 2.0.

Genealogy 2.0

Geneticists have discovered that traumatic events like earthquakes, floods, major climate events, and sociopolitical events like wars, diasporas, and economic crashes—all of these kinds of powerful occurrences have major emotional as well as physical impacts on the people who lived through them.

The emotional reactions, decisions, choices and thoughts your ancestors made in the face of major environmental and social traumas quite literally changed how their genetics were expressed—changes they passed down to you, affecting how you live, think and act to this day.

I'll explain the science of epigenetics (the study of heritable changes in gene expression) behind this phenomenon shortly. But fundamentally, once you can identify past historical events that impacted your ancestors, you have a solid lead on emotional DNA patterns—inherited patterns of thoughts feelings and actions—that might have been passed down to you, causing issues in your own life.

By taking your physical Genealogy 1.0 results and doing a little research into significant social and geographic events that affected your ancestors, and then taking that information and stepping through a process called Systemic Work & Constellations, you can not only discover a whole world of psychological and emotional information about yourself, but you can also actually change emotional DNA patterns and advance your human potential.

You can take your basic genealogy findings (Genealogy 1.0) and research traumatic events that may have impacted the lives of your ancestors (Genealogy 2.0). Then, by applying certain tools and techniques, you can figure out the answers to amazingly detailed questions —like why you overeat or why you have difficulty letting relationships go. You can gain valuable insights into hugely personal issues—like why money always seems to elude you, why you get anxious in social situations, or why lovers always seem to leave.

This is Genealogy 3.0

Genealogy 3.0
Genealogy 3.0 takes all the information acquired in Genealogy 1.0 and Genealogy 2.0 and steps you through a transformative experience that enables you to evolve and grow beyond those limiting inherited issues.

Genealogy 3.0 uses select tools from Systemic Work and Constellations, a process designed to enable you to literally see, hear, feel, identify, interact with and change previously invisible patterns and unconscious loyalties you've inherited from your family lineage and society. A step-by-step process in this book will help you tap into inherited patterns, then show you how to transform those limiting patterns, guiding you through a quick, powerful, and embodied "reframe" of your particular issue(s) or problem(s).

Once a formerly unconscious inherited pattern becomes conscious, you begin to understand not only the suffering, loss or limitations it created, but also the gifts it contained. This can lead to significant shifts in your thoughts, feelings and actions, which, in turn, empower you to start living life in a whole new and more fulfilling way.

Inherited patterns aren't all bad!
It's important to understand that not all inherited emotional DNA patterns are limiting. Some inheritable patterns—like resilience, determination, and a "can do" attitude—are extremely positive. Even if you have inherited limiting patterns of emotional DNA (and we all have!), you need to know that inherited negative emotional DNA patterns are neither destiny nor doom.

They are portals to possibility.

Unlike your physical DNA, which cannot be changed except via genomic surgery, your emotional DNA can be altered. Your family lineage—your ancestral heritage—is a unique living system. And like all other living systems, it has a built-in mandate to change, grow and evolve. And guess who is in charge of your family's physical DNA and emotional DNA evolution? That's right. You!

If the emotional DNA patterns you inherit are healthy ones, say a positive work ethic (so often transmitted down through Northern European and early American genetic lines), or a strong appreciation for family tradition (often transmitted through Asian lineages), that's great. If, however those patterns become limiting—if the strong work ethic has warped into perfectionism or workaholism; if honoring family traditions has turned into crippling conservatism and an inability to break free and shine as your truest self—it's time to understand that those ancestral emotional DNA patterns have outlived their usefulness. What was once a solution for someone (or many someones) in your family line has now become a problem.

The fact that what was once a healthy pattern has now become problematic for you, is a powerful indicator that your family system is evolving. It doesn't matter if everyone else in your family is still happily working themselves to death and feeling miserable. If you find this pattern uncomfortable and desire a more pleasurable kind of life, YOU are the designated family pattern breaker! Quite literally, your entire family system, past, present, and future, is begging you to follow the clues to your discomfort and explore your desire to break the pattern, bringing forth your unique influence and abilities to transform that old ancestral work pattern into something more positive.

    You are the one in the driver's seat. You are the one living on planet Earth right here, right now. You are the one who inherited the exploratory drive that sent your Viking or your Polynesian ancestors roving across the seas. How you express that inherited pattern is entirely up to you. Are you restless as the ocean itself? Never able to settle down to any one thing? Are you driven by curiosity to search the stars for signs of intelligent life, going for a career in astrophysics? Where did that come from and how will you evolve that family pattern?

How does emotional DNA get started?

As I said earlier, your emotional DNA is your inherited patterns of thoughts, feelings, emotions, actions and inactions. Let me give you an example of how an ancestral pattern imprinted on a family system's emotional DNA can outlive its usefulness and be changed.

    A few years ago, Minh, a successful businessman of Vietnamese heritage, came to me complaining about feeling driven to work to the point of collapse. "My grandfather came to the United States from Vietnam during the war," he said. "He and then my father worked three jobs to support the family. I'm doing quite well for myself and my family, but I feel I am not working hard enough. Even though I'm exhausted by day's end, I feel like I should take on another job." He shook his head wearily. "I don't know what to do."

    As we worked through his family pattern, he realized it was just that: A pattern. Taking another job was simply perpetuating the survival pattern of his family system. But his body was saying, "No! Please. Stop! See what's driving you and do life differently!" It was telling him "You're already beyond this pattern."

Working with me, he realized his family system was trying to evolve through him. The time for desperately working hard at any job that came to hand just to survive was past. His grandfather and father had paved the way for him to create a family where success and money had taken root and it was time for some relaxation, appreciation, and play.

I explained that if he didn't shift the work pattern that was, quite literally, killing him, he would just be passing on the pattern to his children. And then the task of changing this pattern would be left to them.

The thought of imposing this on his children created a shift in him. He didn't want to see his children become as tired and despondent as him. To celebrate his considerable economic achievements, instead of taking on another job, he took some of the money he had saved and invested it in a really nice vacation for himself and his family. He invited both his parents and his four grandparents to a big family dinner and honored their hard work by paying off his father's home mortgage and buying new furniture for his grandparents. (Along with a big flatscreen TV!)

The pattern of driven determination and overworking was no longer needed and a new pattern of ease and generosity could begin for both Minh and his descendants.

How can I use Genealogy 3.0?

If you've already had your DNA tested and know where your ancestry lies geographically, great. If not, then get it done. Very few people nowadays have much of an idea about their genetic lineage. Most don't even know their mother's maiden name let alone the kinds of historical and geological events that affected their ancestors further back.

Once you have your genealogical chart, you have the geographic map of your family's past, and you can start to do the research to see what kinds of serious events might have impacted your family line.

If you have family stories that have been passed down— remembered family history to draw on—that is a wonderful help. Perhaps five generations ago your great-great-something grandfather was rumored to be a bit of an adventurer. He moved West from Philadelphia to Chicago and became a real estate speculator (a major 19th century Chicago enterprise). He put everything he had into commercial storefronts. And then along came the Great Chicago Fire of 1871 and wiped the family out. And you wonder why your family is ultraconservative when it comes to business dealings and investments? Well, now you know.

But even if you know nothing of your family history, or if, like Jesse in the opening story, you were adopted, it really doesn't matter. Systemic patterns are passed on to you whether you are conscious of them or not. You have only to watch shows like *Long Lost Family* to see how patterns repeat.

Which means to understand your family patterns, all you have to do is observe your own life.

The patterns of your thoughts, the kinds of thoughts you think, the strength and repetition of your feelings, your desires and fears, your inaction and/or your actions, your choices, addictions, phobias, inexplicable dogmatism—all these things are part of what lives in your system whether you know the particulars of your family history or not.

What situations repeat for you? Where are you consistently stuck? What stories do you tell yourself about your abilities and potential? When you combine these questions with your genetic map and a little research, a whole vista of understanding and transformational opportunity opens up before you.

You may never know which specific ancestor first sparked the patterns of fear and doubt, determination and integrity that live in you. But you will be able to discover events in your genealogical history that may have triggered those emotional DNA patterns. Which means you'll be able to discover, acknowledge and retire the old ancestral emotional DNA patterns that no longer serve, working with them until they evolve into wisdom, fulfillment and new directions.

Courtesy of your lineage, there is the seed of greatness in you, either in collusion with or reaction to your family system. As you sow it and begin to change, not only will you rise and transform, you will also lay down new, healthier, evolutionary patterns for you and your descendants. Those who come after you will be the beneficiaries of your Genealogy 3.0 journey. But it all begins with you.

Now, let's get started!

PART I:

Epigenetics, Brain Plasticity, Identifying & Understanding Ancestral Patterns

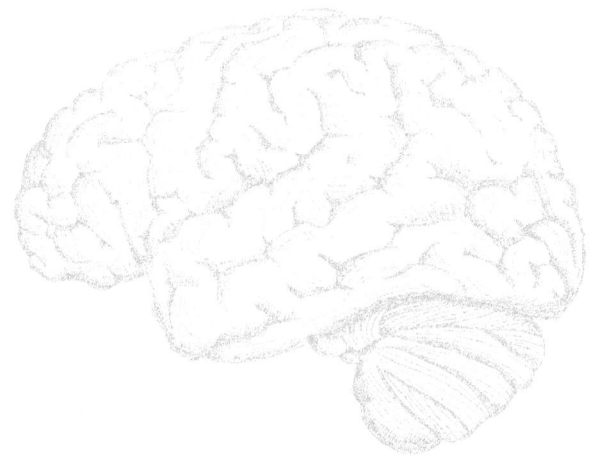

CHAPTER ONE:

A Quick Look at Epigenetics and Brain (Neuro) Plasticity

Diving into Genealogy 3.0, you want to understand how emotions create imprints on your DNA and how those emotional patterns can be passed along to you. You also need to understand a little bit about the neurology of change—how old emotional patterns in you can be transformed by altering your perceptions around any issue you might have, changing your thinking and thus how you've been feeling and acting all your life.

Genealogy 3.0, is about taking old inherited ancestral patterns that are no longer serving you and causing significant changes to happen by literally rewiring your brain. And that can happen over the course of weeks and months, or it can happen in a matter of moments.

But let's start with how emotions create imprints on your DNA in the first place. The first few paragraphs are technical talking about the biology of how it works—after that it's easier going.

Epigenetics

Epigenetics is the study of how events, choices, behaviors and environmental conditions affect us emotionally, and how those emotional reactions affect the way our genes work, *causing changes in gene expression—and thus behaviors*—in subsequent generations.

The first scientific evidence that emotions affect genetic

expression arose after World War II when grandchildren of Holocaust survivors were found to have higher anxiety levels, lower self-esteem, inhibition of aggression and relational difficulties than those found in other children. Studies revealed that the trauma their ancestors experienced may have left chemical markers on their genes, markers that were passed down, resulting in emotional and relational problems.[1]

Since then, clinical studies have linked parental stress to a risk of neurodevelopmental and neuropsychiatric disorders in their children.[2] Animal studies show that epigenetic information is transmitted via the gametes (reproductive cells).[3] Another clinical study shows that lab rats exposed to prenatal stress, maternal separation, abusive caregiving and adult social stress demonstrate epigenetic changes in DNA methylation (a biological process by which methyl groups are added to the DNA molecule), and histone modification (proteins which DNA spools around). There is also evidence that abusive caregiving traits are passed down to both offspring and grand-offspring.[4]

In my own field of Systemic Work and Constellations, studies clearly reveal that human beings tend to pass on traumatic experiences from one generation to the next in family systems. This behavioral continuity shows up in all sorts of ways: anxiety disorders, mood disorders, aggressive behavior, PTSD, social withdrawal and health risk behaviors in the second and third generation.[5]

Similar stressors can trigger epigenetic markers

Emotionally charged events don't change our actual DNA. Instead, they leave "markers" attached to our DNA that alter which proteins are made and thus which genes are *expressed*, turning certain genes "on" and "off" in response to environmental factors in our lives. When we experience stress, fatigue, abuse, and impactful situations similar to those our ancestors were exposed to, it affects how our body reads our genes and those markers, triggering a matching expression of a DNA sequence.

Let's say you're under a lot of stress at work. Suddenly,

inexplicably, you start feeling paranoid about the overall security of your life and the lives of your family. You spend sleepless nights in terror for your wellbeing. Where did this new and powerful emotion come from? You may be expressing an ancestral pattern—an emotion or a choice or a reaction—that was set in motion in response to similar stress-filled events generations earlier.

Let's look at another example. Let's say your great-grandmother lived through what's known as the Great Dutch Hunger Winter in the Netherlands between 1944-45, barely surviving by supplementing scanty rations with rats and tulip bulbs. (Those were indeed two of the most reliable food staples in Holland during that time.) Women who were pregnant during this famine had children who suffered with weight problems later in life. Depending on when in the pregnancy a lack of nutrition occurred, offspring experienced either obesity or an inability to gain sufficient weight throughout their lives.[6] But the interesting thing is, some studies show that weight problems—both obesity and underweight issues—plagued the grandchildren as well.[7] They also experienced higher rates of conditions like diabetes and schizophrenia, and, on average, died younger than their peers.[8]

Of course, the grandkids didn't have a clue why they had an eating disorder or why they felt anxious all the time. They thought it was all *their* fault. About the last thing they and their parents and their therapists would ever think is that they inherited an eating disorder and anxiety from Grandma or Grandpa. But they did.

Reacting to various stimuli in your life, the epigenetic markers laid down in your DNA (as a result of experiences your ancestors had) trigger the expression of inherited feelings, language, choices, and actions in <u>you</u>, affecting everything from your food preferences to your fashion sense to your preference for a dark-haired mate.

For example, in April 2010, Hollywood actress Brooke Shields went on the TV show *Who Do You Think You Are?* All her life, Brooke had believed her ancestry was Italian. Yet all her life she'd been fascinated by French culture and was puzzled by the attraction. She took French in school, then went on to study French literature at Princeton. She even decorated her home with French furniture from the era of Louis XIV. Then she went on the show and discovered that her family roots went back to France and not Italy like she'd always been told!

I see clients repeat ancestral patterns in many areas, including relationships, success, purpose, fears, dreams, finances, leadership and health. I can hear emotional DNA markers in the unique and often idiosyncratic words and language that clients speak. I see these markers in the unwritten, yet clearly understood, survival-based rules that run the family systems of which they are a part.

A family pattern of quiet invisibility
Here's a simple example of epigenetic inheritance. "Aaron" came to me because his job in advertising, which he clearly loved, was suffering from his lack of participation at creative meetings. "I've got all these ideas," he said, "But when it comes time to share them, it's like this weight of silence comes over me and I can't speak. It's weird—almost like somebody has their hand over my mouth."

When we dove into Aaron's ancestry, it came as no surprise that his family was Jewish. His great-grandfather and his aunt had been hidden in a neighbor's basement for over a year after his parents were snatched by Nazi occupiers in Austria. Their very lives had depended upon invisibility, silence and never speaking up—an unconscious pattern that was still showing up three generations later.

It's nature AND nurture
With epigenetics, nature and nurture come together. We have the genes we've inherited from our ancestors, but *how* they express depends on what's around us, how we are nurtured (or not) and, most importantly, the meaning we have made of what surrounds and affects us and our response to it.

In Aaron's case, his livelihood depended upon being gregarious and easily sharing ideas and being noticed. Yet, to his surprise he found he couldn't easily do it. The more nervous he became over keeping his job, the more he unconsciously moved deeper and deeper into a survival-based situation. That environment stimulated the expression of an emotional DNA marker from his grandfather whose survival had depended upon silence. Talk about a conflict between genetics and environment!

The good news is *epigenetic effects can be changed.* When you intentionally rewire your patterns of thoughts, feelings and actions, your brain and your reality are literally no longer the same … and neither is your ancient history or hitherto predictable future. When you finally identify, acknowledge, and change old family patterns that are still echoing through you, the door to the remarkable opens and you are able to generate, experience and embody an evolutionary leap.

So, just how many generations are affected by traumatic events? How far back does this emotional DNA inheritance go? Is it possible your fear of loud noises and hemophobia (fear of blood) go all the way back to some dim, distant ancestor who fought in the Battle of Hastings in 1066, when William Duke of Normandy (aka William the Conqueror) conquered the English army, beginning the Norman Conquest of England?

Nobody knows the answer to this question yet. But practitioners in Systemic Work and Constellations—including myself—have observed patterns going back seven generations. I remember several years ago a man came to me with a truly peculiar concern. He was terrified that he'd lose one of his legs by the time he was 55-years old—a horrifying experience that had happened to the eldest male in his family for seven generations in a row. One man had lost a leg in a sawmill accident, one in a car wreck, one in a mining explosion, one in World War II etc.

I explained to him that he was in the grip of an ancestral pattern and talked about how patterns and the emotions attached to them are passed down epigenetically. I also explained the power of belief and the power of emotions. When he finally "got" that he was dealing with a pattern and not "fate" itself, that he wasn't cursed and destined to lose a leg, he started to let go his fear. He broke the family pattern and today, at age 63, he still has both his legs!

Again, no one knows how long these emotional DNA patterns can be passed along. But considering the fact that no generation so far in human history has been spared war, famine, pestilence, floods, fires, and economic disasters, the "knock-on effect" where old traumas are triggered over and over again down through the generations, keeping negative, stress-induced emotional DNA patterns alive seems pretty likely.

Neuroplasticity and the dawn of new hope
Up until the early 21st century, most doctors and researchers believed that the human brain was "hard wired" by the time we were in our twenties. They firmly believed that everybody's thoughts and beliefs were almost impossible to change after that. (You could say their belief was "hardwired" and inflexible too!) Looking around at most of humanity, this belief made a lot of sense because most people seem to become more inflexible as they age.

But this is just one way of looking at it. In truth, what's happening is that as they get older, most people tend to become more loyal to the patterns they have inherited—and more comfortable living within their limitations.

The brain is actually highly flexible at any point in life. As far back as 1949, the "father of neuroscience," Santiago Ramón y Cajal, discovered that non-pathological changes could—and often did—take place in the neurological structure of adult brains. He dubbed this ability of the brain to change in a healthy way as "neuronal plasticity," later dubbed "brain plasticity."

In the 1960s, Canadian psychologist Donald Hebb discovered that neurons in the adult brain adapt during any sort of learning process. This is why a lot of doctors recommend that seniors take up new studies or learn a new language. It keeps their brains flexible. He famously taught that new neuron patterns form based upon associated thoughts and that "Neurons wire together if they fire together."

Studies now show that new neural pathways in the brain can be formed over a period of about 21 days, with the new behavior becoming automatic after about ten to twelve weeks. Which is wonderful news! Having a dynamic, living, changing brain that responds to new thoughts and experiences throughout one's lifespan offers the doorway to an ongoing adventure.

So, how does neuroplasticity work? Let's say you were badly scratched by a cat when you were three-years old. New neural pathways are formed very quickly when strong emotions occur in moments of pain and fear. During highly traumatic events, our brains operate at hyper-speed. If a situation is intense enough and/or repeated often enough, we lay down a new neural pattern around the event. In this particular case, the pattern that starts to become wired in the brain is "Cat's are dangerous hurtful things."

Now you get scared every time you see a cat. If that fear response pattern isn't interrupted—if Mommy or Daddy doesn't sit you down with a friendly feline and teach you that all cats aren't scary—your brain can become so hair-trigger primed around associating cats with pain and fear, that you even begin to experience a fear response to *pictures* of cats. And then you pass that fear on to your own children and pretty soon no one in the family likes cats anymore.

This kind of neurological pattern-making happens all the time, especially under highly emotional conditions both positive and negative, reactive or creative. For example, as a kid maybe you forgot your lines in the Halloween play in first grade and the other kids laughed at you. Ever since then you've had performance anxiety when you're singled out to do something in front of an audience. But years later another equally emotional experience comes along.

You're playing in a high school basketball tournament. The score is tied. It's the end of the game and you get fouled. Up to the free throw line you go, nervous as can be. And you make the shot! You win the game! The crowd goes wild! Your teammates go wild. Your coach goes wild. Your parents are jumping up and down in the stands waving and cheering. It's an emotional success moment you never forget. It gets stamped on your genes and overwrites the old performance anxiety pattern. From then on, even though you might still be nervous, you have confidence going into tight, stressful situations where most people melt.

Habitual thinking is addictive

It becomes incredibly easy to think the same thoughts and experience the same emotions over and over about the world, about certain people, situations, ideas, and beliefs. By the time we're in our thirties we almost don't have to think at all. Our brains easily go on automatic and fire the same old thoughts and feelings about the neighbors, our ex, money, work, the last election, and on and on.

These habitual mental patterns and their accompanying emotions biochemically "mark" our genes and end up being passed down through the generations. (Maybe that basketball player's kids end up being cool as cucumbers in high-stress positions.) Just like our ancestors experienced emotional stuff that ended up creating the patterns *we* inherited, we do the same thing and pass patterns on down to *our* descendants.

Fortunately, neuroplasticity guarantees we can change our brains, change our thoughts, change our emotions and literally change the way our genes express, saving our great-great grandkids from inheriting our issues. And we can change the patterns that were passed down to us.

Let me give you an example of how quickly you can change an inherited ancestral pattern using Genealogy 3.0. "Terry" came to an event of mine because she felt isolated and alone. Even though she was raised in a family with several brothers and sisters, she said she always felt like the "odd person out." This same pattern of exclusion was beginning to affect her work. She'd been passed over for promotion a couple of times because her bosses felt she just didn't connect well with her co-workers.

"Were you left alone a lot growing up?" I asked.

"No," Terry said. "I had a pretty regular upbringing. Our parents loved us and they were home every night. Nobody deliberately left me out of things. I did it to myself, I guess. It seems like I spent most of my teen years in my bedroom while the rest of the family played games or watched TV together."

After some more questioning, we set up something called

a "constellation," a process that enables you to physically create a three-dimensional representation of an issue using other people (or even pieces of paper or figurines) to represent family members and various aspects of whatever issue you're working on.

Terry selected 14 other workshop members to stand in as her family members, arranging each person in the room in a way that "felt" right to her. Here's a diagram of Terry's family constellation and the positions they held standing in the room:

TERRY

TERRY'S CONSTELLATION

TERRY'S GRANDMOTHER

Just like star constellations in the sky have a unique pattern of stars, so every family system has a unique pattern reflecting how a person perceives their family members relate to each other. As you can see from Terry's constellation and how she's placed herself in relation to everybody in her family, she sees herself as separate from her parents and siblings. All her mother's siblings (Terry's aunts and uncles) are grouped close together as well. But Terry's grandmother—her mom's mother—stands out, isolated from the rest of the family, just like Terry.

When Terry looked at the 3-dimensional representation of her family, it hit her. "Oh, my goodness!" she gasped, eyes huge as saucers as she glanced back and forth between her "grandmother" standing alone outside the constellation with all the other family representative standing snuggly close together.

"What?" I prompted.

Tears starting in her eyes, she whispered, "Grandma was ... alone."

"What happened that she was so alone?" I prompted.

"Her husband drowned. He was a fisherman." Terry frowned. "I never met her ... she was my mom's mom and she died about five or six years after my mother was born."

"What else do you know about your grandmother's aloneness?" I asked.

Terry hesitated. "Mom said her mother started drinking after her husband died. She'd hide up in her bedroom, alone. There were a lot of kids—mom has eight siblings. She was the baby, born a few months after Grandpa died. All the kids had to just raise themselves."

"What happened to your grandmother?" I asked. "Do you know?"

"It was really awful," Terry said. "My mom told me her mom just wandered off one night drunk. They found her body beside the road a few days later."

Quite a dramatic story! You can probably already see where Terry's isolation pattern came from, can't you? So, how did Terry resolve her issue? How did she "rewire" the isolation pattern running (and ruining) her life? Frankly, more than half the transformation was her seeing the inherited pattern. The shock of recognition was enormous. When she realized the pattern that had run her life wasn't *hers*, her entire perception of her issue and her life instantly changed in what is called a "mental reframe."

"Oh, my goodness!" she gasped. "You mean I'm not, weird or messed up or something?"

I assured her that the pattern was, indeed, not her. I had already explained the science of epigenetics and how emotional patterns are passed down from generation to generation. So, she "got it." Then we took a few more steps toward closure.

After some coaching from me, Terry walked up to the woman representing her grandmother and said, "Nobody in the family has seen you for a long, long time. But *I see you.* I see how painful losing Grandpa was for you. I see how you couldn't stay with the family and belong, *But I can belong*. I see you and I will leave this pain and exclusion with you.

"Thank you for showing me what happens when you close your heart, shut down and isolate. I am going to do life differently and open my heart to others and live the full life that you could not. I will take my place and be seen" And then she added, "There will always be a place for you in our family and in my heart."

Later, Terry talked about her "aha" to the group. She said it felt as though a huge burden had been lifted off her heart. She shared how excited she was at the thought of living life truly engaged with other people rather than suffering from chronic isolation.

About a year after the event, she called to tell me about a huge promotion at work and how she had pole vaulted past several other people in the running for the position. "They told me I got the job because of my ability to pull people together and create a sense of belonging!" she laughed. "Imagine that!"

This is how plastic our brains are. This is how rapidly and completely we can change and heal when we finally understand what's going on in our lives and what patterns are running the show.

The winner's edge

Athletes do this all the time. The brain has a peculiar way of not being able to tell the difference between an actual physical experience and simply *imagining* that same experience. Athletes practice visualizing, feeling, and experiencing an athletic performance in their minds over and over again, laying down the neural patterns of a perfect performance in their brains. Then they go out and physically achieve the remarkable. *Because they have already done it in their minds!*

You are in a powerful position to change and evolve into the fullest version of the unique individual you were born to be—no matter what patterns you have inherited or created!

QUICK CONSTELLATION EXERCISE

Write the names of each of your family members on a piece of paper: Mom, Dad, siblings, grandparents (on both sides) and aunts, uncles, cousins (if they're close enough).

Now, lay out the pieces of paper on the floor or a table top in a way that shows how you see the family members relating to each other. Let's say your mom and dad are really distant from one another and fight a lot. But your dad is close to your sister and you're close to your mom. Also, your mom is super close with *her* mom.

EXAMPLE CONSTELLATION

In this example, the pieces of paper with your parents' names wouldn't be close together. But the pieces of paper with Mom written on it and Grandma would be close together. Etc.

So, what possible personal issue might be reflected within this constellation?

Well, maybe you have a repetitive thought along the lines of "No man can be trusted." This thought has been responsible for the break up of every intimate relationship you've ever had. And when you see this constellation and see how close your mom and grandma are—and how your grandmother energetically stands between your mother and your father—you suddenly realize, "Wow! Grandma used to say men couldn't be trusted! That's because Grandpa ran off with his secretary. And she used to say that to mom all the time. And mom never trusted my dad—which is why they're not close. And I unconsciously inherited that same thought!"

See how this works?

So, lay out your family's constellation. After you've arranged all the pieces of paper in a way that feels/seems right to you, stand back and look at the pattern. Does anything come up for you? Does the pattern you're seeing "ring any bells?"

Later in the book I'll coach you through the creation of a 3D constellation based on a particular issue you want to address and heal. But perhaps you can already see how useful this technique is for creating an opportunity to see, hear, touch, feel and literally *walk through* any story that goes on inside your head, thus experiencing the issue and its possible resolution from a completely different physiological perspective?

CHAPTER TWO:

How to Know You're Entangled in a Multi-generational Pattern

"Jack" came to me at his wife's request. He was 50 years old and struggling with weight issues that had plagued him all his life. He also had a bad hoarding habit. The ultimatum came when boxes of "stuff," stacked floor to ceiling in the garage, fell on his wife while she was inching her way through his "collection" trying to get to the washing machine.

"She said unless I clean out the garage and the rest of the house she's leaving," he said miserably. "I know it's crazy. But something in me just panics at the idea of getting rid of anything. What if I need it someday?" He shook his head. "I don't know why I can't let stuff go. But I just can't. What's *wrong* with me?"

When I started asking Jack questions about his immediate family, there didn't seem to be any obvious reasons for his problems. Growing up, his family had been relatively well-off and stable. His father had been a residential building contractor who made good money in the post World War II building boom. His mother he described as a "bit of a flake." Like Jack, both his older sisters were overweight and liked "to collect things." This had been the case ever since he could remember.

This was my first clue that a family pattern was involved. When the same issue manifests in multiple family members, or multiple generations of family members, there is a strong possibility that a multigenerational pattern is in play, expressing through those symptoms. In Jack's case, the pattern was excess weight and hoarding.

Now, patterns are present in a family for two reasons: 1) So the people or events that are excluded can finally take their place and unresolved issues can be resolved and 2) to point you squarely towards your own purpose and destiny. I started asking Jack questions designed to reveal the patterns driving his unwanted habits.

"Tell me about your mom," I asked. "Why do you call her a flake?"

Jack shrugged. "I don't know. She had a real restlessness about her. A resistance to being settled in one place, doing one thing."

"Did she try to hold onto things?" I asked.

"No. If anything, she was the exact opposite."

"Did she make you get rid of stuff all the time?" I asked, thinking we might be getting somewhere.

"No. Not really. She didn't mind if I collected stuff as long as I kept my room neat."

"What about meals? What were your parents' attitudes about food?"

"Dad didn't much care as long as there was cold beer in the fridge when he came home from work. Mom?" he shrugged. "She was an okay cook, I guess."

"Did you always have enough to eat?"

He looked startled. "Yeah. Of course, we did. Food just was never a big issue." He stopped. "Well, hm. Now that I think about it, mom was super weight conscious. And ... we never had sweets around or anything. I remember my sisters and I used to hoard candy and any other sweet we could get our hands on." His voice dropped to a shamed whisper. "I used to guard my stash and gobble it up quickly so my sisters wouldn't steal it."

So, there was a bit of a pattern of hoarding around food, a pattern a number of different kinds of events can trigger, imprinting our DNA. He didn't know much about his grandparents on either side of the family. He thought maybe his grandmother on his mother's side had immigrated from Albania. Or maybe her parents. He didn't know. His genealogical chart showed close to 90 percent of his DNA came from Eastern Europe, which supported his guess. The rest was mostly Southern European and Caucasus regions.

"Grandma—mom's mom—was huge," he said.

"Was she a hoarder?"

"I don't remember." His jaw dropped. "But I do recall her looking at me one day and saying in this thick accent, 'Let me tell you Djalë. At the end of life, all that's left of you are your things. They are your whole life story. Don't ever let that go.'"

And there it was.

Looking at the history of Albania, from 1770 up to World War I, the country was plagued by constant wars, mostly with the Ottoman Empire. The mid-nineteenth century was marked by one revolt after another, and the population was under heavy strife, plagued with critical food shortages and just about every other kind of shortage. Between 1891 and 1910, over 12 million people emigrated to the United States, mostly from Eastern Europe, among them, most likely, Jack's great-grandparents on his mother's side.

They brought next to nothing with them except a lineage of upheaval, fear, and constant loss—loss of food, loss of home, loss of possessions, loss of personal and national identity. It was this family pattern of loss, and the fear of loss, that Jack inherited. The pattern showed up in his hoarding of things he "might need someday" and in his overeating. (Logically, overeating sometimes happens when there is a deep unconscious fear around food not being available.) This family fear was never discussed or even recognized. It just cropped up in odd ways, like in his grandmother's weight problem and her comment about the importance of holding onto things.

So, why didn't this pattern show up in his mother?

Well, sometimes patterns skip generations. But if they aren't recognized, acknowledged, and resolved, they reappear. In systems, everything belongs and has a place, and what is excluded will always resurface somewhere somehow. But, if you think about it, Jack's mother was also marked by this lack/fear/holding-on dynamic. She just handled it in the opposite way from her mother, Jack and his sisters. She refused to overeat, refused to settle down and refused to hold onto things, actually stepping towards creating a different emotional DNA pattern from her mother and grandparents.

The problem was, *his mother didn't do this consciously, so the change didn't register and couldn't be used as the gift that it was*. She was just as enmeshed in the family "fear/hold on/don't let go" pattern, and just as run by it. The pattern simply showed up in her as rejection/opposition. She did not see and consciously resolve the issue. She didn't consciously evolve the family's emotional DNA. She simply pushed food and things *away* in response to the fear of loss she sensed in her mother and grandparents.

Now, here is where things get really exciting with Genealogy 3.0.

When Jack realized that his problem of overeating and hoarding was actually a pattern passed down from his Eastern European ancestors, it stopped being "his" problem. This kind of new view on an issue is what is known as a "systemic insight and reframe." I remember Jack's face and how he looked when this new point of view hit him.

"It's not *my* issue! It's not *me!*" He sat there for a few minutes, eyes wide, obviously chewing on this brand-new thought. "I'm not a stupid, greedy person!" He heaved a great sigh, rolling his eyes in astonished relief. "It's just a pattern showing up *through* me. And I can choose how I respond to the pattern, right? I can figure out what to do with it?"

"Absolutely," I told him. "This pattern is a part of you and it simply wants to be given its place, just like all things do in systems. Once you acknowledge it and give it a place, you no longer need to carry it. You have a choice. You can change your thoughts, feelings and actions around this."

I then guided Jack through a process that I will teach you later, a process that enabled him to transform this ancestral loss pattern by 1) acknowledging the pattern, 2) giving it a place in the family system, 3) finding the gift in the pattern, 4) re-languaging his thinking about loss, hoarding and food, and then 5) pivoting—investing in his new view, his new dreams and the new life waiting for him.

Bottom line, if you're a human being and alive, family patterns in the form of emotional DNA are alive and happening within you. Whether or not certain patterns are unconsciously running your life in limiting or even positive ways, *that's* the question you want to answer. If they are limiting, you want to learn how to change them. The first step in this process is learning how to know if an ancestral pattern is in play, and then determining whether it is healthy or unhealthy

Ancestral pattern identifiers: clues to ancestral patterns in your system

- **Repeating family patterns**

One of the easiest ways to tell if you're stuck in an inherited emotional DNA pattern is to look around and see if anybody else in the family is exhibiting or did exhibit the same pattern or some version of it. For example, in the story above, Jack and his sisters all had the same issues around weight.

Of course, not all family patterns are that obvious. Plus, not all family patterns have the same symptomology. Just like different people catching the same flu bug might have different symptoms, so family members embodying the same emotional DNA pattern might reveal it differently. Take a family pattern of perfectionism, for example.

Let's say your grandfather was a doctor—a brain surgeon. Perfectionism is an important trait for a brain surgeon to develop. Right? Or maybe he was a Colonel in the Army or Airforce. Everything always had to be spic and span and orderly. The kids grew up in rooms that looked like they were in military school—no mess, not a toy out of place. Good grades were a must. Obedience was a given. Etc.

In both cases, grandfather's perfectionism was a healthy thing because the lives of patients and soldiers under his care were on the line. Which doesn't mean it was easy on his kids. But they grew up healthy and relatively happy with a good work ethic and prospered. After they got married and had kids, unsurprisingly they also ran their households in a perfectionist kind of way.

However, let's say one of their kids, a grandchild of the third generation, slides into drug use to compensate for the constant pressure the perfectionist pattern exerts on him or her. Or perhaps the straight-A grandchild lives up to the perfection model on the outside, but meanwhile spends nights in the bathroom carefully cutting his or herself where the marks can't be seen by others.

For two generations, the pattern of perfectionism worked and there was no reason for the pattern to shift. However, when self-destructive behaviors show up in reaction to a pattern (perfectionism is just one of many possibilities), the symptoms themselves may be pointing to one of two things: 1) The pattern has outlived its usefulness, is becoming a problem and needs to change. 2) Something or someone has been excluded causing an imbalance in the system that needs to be addressed. (I explain this a little further down under the heading "You feel excluded or feel like something or someone is missing in your life," and in the next chapter under "Belonging.")

In this case, instead of keeping people alive, perfectionism is now eroding the mental and physical health of some family members. In other words, the child and the family system as a whole have arrived at the point where it is time to change that pattern. With gratitude for the gifts it brought, perfectionism needs to be acknowledged as a tool that helped a family system thrive and become all it could be ... until it no longer served and perhaps flexibility becomes a welcome partner.

Main Point: <u>The pattern has to be seen and understood in order for the mindsets and patterns of thoughts, feelings and actions to be transformed.</u>

Let's say you've got an issue around not being able to save money. You earn a good living, but no matter how hard you try, money slips through your fingers. By the end of every month, you're sweating bullets, trying to figure out how to make ends meet. Look around at other family members. Is there anyone else in your family or family line with money issues?

Maybe your brother is a tightwad? Or a wealthy workaholic trying to make sure the money flow is constant? Maybe Mom compulsively saves coins. Everything goes in the penny jar, but nothing ever comes out. Not having money seems to be a theme. Think about it. Then go and investigate your genealogy. Is there a specific event that may have triggered that pattern in your ancestral line? Did someone way back lose the family fortune? Rob a bank and go to jail? Make terrible investments in the stock market? Live in a war-torn nation filled with shortages and economic deprivation?

- **You exhibit noticeable patterns around specific areas**

I've already touched on one specific area. Money! But there are plenty of other subjects that end up creating issues (or opportunities), creating inheritable family patterns via emotional DNA. How about sex? Intimacy? Relationship? Success? Business? Power? Leadership? Happiness? Health? Prejudice? Racism?

It's pretty much a rule of thumb: If you have an ongoing issue with something, it's in response to a pattern.

If you experience a driving passion to move in a new direction, it's in response to a pattern. And whatever the pattern is, it can lock you up in all kinds of ways until you see it, acknowledge it, find the gift in it, reframe it and use the reframe to create the next healthy, conscious pattern and climb the next wonderful and exciting step.

Do you find yourself chafing under a boss at work? Can s/he do nothing right in your eyes? Do you feel resentful of any authority? Are you constantly criticizing the "powers that be?" Always finding fault? Do you feel angry about how the world is being run to the point you lose sleep over it? There's a pattern there crying out to be transformed. *By you!* Can't get ahead at work no matter how hard you try? Does success constantly elude you?

There's another pattern crying out to be transformed.

Do a quick check in with other family members and see if your issue is shared. But whether it is or isn't, realize that change is in your own hands. And don't be dismayed. You're looking squarely in the face of opportunity!

- **You react to certain things disproportionally**

Being easily triggered by specific things—dogs, criticism, being ignored, loud noises—is an excellent indicator that you've got an ancestral pattern showing up.

- **Your language is inflated, diminished, or strangely themed**

If you find yourself exaggerating, minimizing, or using variations of the same words and phrases, or have the same, exaggeratedly-themed thoughts, look to see how they might be pointing toward some sort of impactful event in your family line. For example, I had a client, a woman who had emigrated to the US from Mexico at an early age. She came to me because she was restless and felt driven to be constantly active.

As we talked, she consistently used fire imagery. She said things like, "I'm burning with anxiety!" and "That idea was burned into my brain." She described her boss's criticism as "searing" and said she had a "scorching desire" to "move at speed" and find a new position.

When I pointed out her strange word choices, she started crying. Turns out, she and her mother had outrun pyroclastic flows from the violent eruption of El Chichon near their village of Francisco Leon in 1982. Her brother and father had been killed, along with over a thousand other villagers. She'd been eight at the time, and until I mentioned her use of language, she had never spoken of the event, even with her mother.

The unacknowledged, unexamined trauma of that event was behind her chronic anxiety and the need to be moving and doing all the time. It was screaming for attention through her language choices. An emotional DNA pattern in the making—a pattern that may well have ended up being passed down to her children and then *their* children and on and on—she had the good fortune to see the unconscious pattern that was building in her and change it.

- **You are illogically or unreasonably dogmatic about certain things**

You refuse to have children. Why? You've just always had a "feeling" that children would not only end life as you know it, having a child might end your very life. So—which ancestor in your family had something similar happen to them? Who died in childbirth?

Or perhaps you have a stubborn streak as wide as the Grand Canyon. If anybody tells you to do something, you can't help but go in the exact opposite direction. Who in your family heritage was forced to do something against their will? Or perhaps they did something that was contrary to the way the family behaved and were excluded from the family itself. Are you unconsciously identified with that person, running their pattern? Or perhaps determined to *not* repeat it?

- **You feel run by an emotion that feels like it doesn't belong to you or has no rational explanation for its existence.**

This is subtler than the other emotional DNA indicators. Let's say you had a nice average upbringing. You weren't abused. You've led a decent life, but deep down there's a simmering rage in you that you're always afraid will boil up and spill over. There's no apparent reason for it. But there it is. And you've spent your whole life tippytoeing around people and situations, hoping that the pot won't explode.

What past ancestor or ancestors experienced abuse? Unfair treatment? Was blamed for something terrible that they didn't do? The unacknowledged event and pattern are still in the family system, making themselves known through you, waiting to be acknowledged and transformed.

- **You don't/can't feel an emotion that seems appropriate**

Let's use the rage example again. Let's say you've experienced abuse. Maybe you were sexually traumatized as a child. Maybe your wife ran away with the yoga instructor, leaving you with five young children to raise. Maybe you're accused of something at work and fired unjustly without any recourse. Anger and rage are appropriate emotions to feel and express in these circumstances, but you just *can't*. You're completely detached from the feeling.

Again, there's a pattern here waiting to be uncovered and a corner turned in your life, freeing you up to be able to fully express. Who else in your family system might have had something happen to them that caused a rage they had to bottle up? Or perhaps they expressed such rage that it alienated them from the rest of the family. Remember too, if *you* don't feel, acknowledge and resolve the pattern, someone further down the family tree will have to deal with it—perhaps one of your children or grandchildren.

- **Someone/something is not spoken of in your family system yet you express it**

Secrets have a way of surfacing because they, too, are part of the system. (Check out the Walt Disney film *Encanto* for a perfect example of this dynamic.)

When a secret remains unaddressed and unresolved, it surfaces in patterns of behavior. Let's say grandma had a secret abortion. No one ever speaks of it. Most people in the family know nothing about it. But there is a sadness and a sense of sexual shame and guilt that women throughout the family line carry in them. They don't talk about it and wonder why they feel that way. Perhaps they even carry a fear of getting pregnant and wonder why.

This is a perfect example of a deep dark secret triggering emotional DNA that gets passed down through the generations.

- **You feel excluded or feel like something or someone is missing in your life**

When family members go missing for whatever reason—a miscarriage, an abortion, an early death, a child adopted out, a brother who died—this creates an invisible imprint on the family system that can show up in the wildest ways. For example, say you have a child who always wants their toys or their food in perfect order. S/he consistently throws an inexplicably violent tantrum when things seem out of order.

This can actually indicate a family member that the child unconsciously senses is missing. Their frantic, apparently unreasonable attempts to give everything their place is an attempt to fill the gap so that they can feel comfortable knowing *their* own place.

Here's a real-life example. I had a client come to me because for the seventh time in seven years, a fast-growing, non-cancerous tumor had bloated her abdomen into a mock pregnancy. Her doctors were clueless as to the cause and so was she. However, when we worked together, she discovered that her grandmother had had seven miscarriages! No one in the family ever spoke about any of those lost babies. Their incomplete lives were completely unacknowledged and ignored. They were a part of the family system, and they were being excluded.

As strange as it might sound (and I've seen this dynamic happen over and over again) what is excluded in a family system usually finds a way to appear elsewhere in the system so it can be acknowledged and finally *consciously* find its place.

When my client acknowledged those seven lost babies and talked about them with the rest of the family, each one of those seven beings was given their place in the family system. After she did this, the seventh tumor rapidly shrank without any need for surgery, and she experienced no more tumors after that. Hard to believe? I agree. And yet it happened.

Or let's say you're unusually passionate about inclusivity issues around certain demographics. Or you're the kind of person who goes out of their way to always make sure everybody feels included in activities. This is another unconscious way of resolving an exclusion. Until it's made conscious, the pattern will persist.

EXERCISE

Think about your life. Is there a pattern you can see repeating? Relationships that continually disappoint? Can't ever seem to do or be enough? Is there a habit you just can't seem to kick? Do you hit the same brick wall over and over again? Or have a place where you feel woefully inadequate? Do you wish things could be different and think they can't change?

Ask yourself:
- When did this thought/feeling/habit begin for me?
- What was happening in my life at the time? What did I make it mean about me? What did I make it mean about others?
- Is there a start point or event you can pinpoint?
- Are there other family members who seem stuck in the same pattern?
- Ask yourself the question: "Is this really mine?"
- Does the pattern serve you? Is there some (not necessarily healthy) benefit you're getting out of it?
- Are you ready to move out of this stuck place? Remember, patterns evolve just like people. Are you the change agent this pattern has been waiting for?

Don't be afraid to ask your family about the patterns you experience. The reason patterns sometimes take so long to resolve is family members often keep patterns of thoughts, feelings and actions to themselves out of embarrassment, guilt, unworthiness or confusion. By doing this we miss the world of clues that are available to us to resolve our issues when they come up.

CHAPTER THREE:

How Ancestral Patterns Affect Us

Now that you know emotional DNA and ancestral patterns exist and have an idea of how to detect them, let's detail the different areas of life that these patterns can affect. Which is pretty much everything, everywhere! Ancestral patterns color our relationships, our health and happiness, business and career, success and failure and, of course, money and how it flows or doesn't flow through our lives.

But before we get into specific areas of impact, I need to briefly introduce you to the three main principles we use in Systemic Work and Constellations—the three main organizing principles found within every system on the planet, including your ancestral system, cultures, nations and ethnicities.

The Three Principles
The three principles at work in every system are 1) belonging, 2) the balance of give and receive, and 3) order/place. Behind every limiting issue plaguing every human being on the planet lies misperceptions, misalignments, meaning making and/or trauma around one or more of these three principles. Within every great success these three principles are also at play.

- **Belonging**

It may not always feel like it, but it is impossible to not belong to your family system. Even if you were left in a basket on the orphanage steps when you were two hours old, you belong in your family system. You are part of that system whether anybody even knows about your existence or not.

Let's continue with the abandonment theme. Will issues around belonging arise in you and the family system if you were abandoned as a baby? Quite possibly, yes. You may well feel like you don't belong anywhere or are never chosen. You may feel lost at sea and left out in the cold. Running this pattern of "not belonging" you may struggle to form healthy relationships with others. Or, understanding the pain of feeling excluded, you may very well turn into the one who includes everybody and creates spaces where everyone can belong. Some great leaders were forged from this kind of belonging issue.

Please remember that a system is the sum of ALL its members, known and unknown, seen and unseen. When you are excluded, the rest of the family system is also impacted. A family member exists (you!), but is MIA. There is a hole that other family members may well try unconsciously to fill. Remember the story of the woman with seven tumors. There were seven missing babies in her family system. Seven holes. Seven "belonging gaps," at play that directly affected her until those gaps were acknowledged and thus filled.

Every system has its own intelligence and its own natural desire to be healthy and evolve. That is the dynamic we see at play.

Here is another aspect of belonging. Perhaps everybody in your nuclear family eats junk food and smokes cigarettes and in order to belong you start doing those same things. You may fear you will be excluded or made fun of if you don't join in. But here's the thing. If you really don't want to eat that way or smoke or engage in other family habits, *you are the change maker.* What's happening is that you are the vehicle the family system is using to expand the health of the family system (literally) as well as expanding ways to belong in your family system. If you follow what feels right for you, you may feel alone for a while. But once you change, others may end up changing in healthy ways too.

- **Balance of give and receive**

We all know how it feels when the scales are tipped. Either we give too much and receive too little. Or we receive/take too much and give too little. We are raised to believe that it's more blessed to give than to receive. And yet have you noticed how somebody who shows appreciation and joy for a gift receives more? There's not a family relationship, intimate relationship, friend relationship, or business relationship where this principle doesn't apply.

When things are out of balance, there is a restlessness or sense of either not doing your fair share or being taken advantage of. It helps to remember two things here. 1) If you aren't doing what you deem your fair share, there's an opportunity to step up and add value. 2) Balance of give and receive has both long and short cycles. You don't want to play "tick the box" to make sure it's all fair and square. Sometimes someone may do something for you and years later it's their turn to ask for your help. Then there are situations where balance isn't easily possible. How do you balance for the gift of life itself? Or the learning you receive from a teacher or mentor? Or a family member who gifted you a life-saving kidney? Sometimes things can't be balanced ... but they can be paid forward!

- **Order/Place**

Order in family systems refers to the order in which people are conceived or born. Just because someone was born first and is oldest doesn't make them better than those who are younger and born second, third, fourth, etc. It just means they arrived first. And remember, just because a child didn't make it all the way into physical life doesn't mean their place doesn't exist. Ignoring the existence of such a being and their place can make everybody else in the family line feel out of order or leave them looking for something that "feels missing." (IE. They're unconsciously looking for what's been excluded.)

When someone is "out of order" in a family system (or a business or political system), issues arise. For example, let's say you're the only child of alcoholic parents. You grew up having to look out for yourself and them. You were the responsible one. In essence, you became the parent, which means you are *out of the proper order* and flow of things in your family system.

Your father and mother came before you. Life, love, and resources (hopefully) flow from them to you. It is their job to care for you, not vice versa. Now, as an adult, you demonstrate this out of order dynamic in your life. You go out in the world and automatically assume too much responsibility. You take on jobs at work that don't belong to you and you annoy your bosses. You take on the responsibility for making your intimate relationship work. As a result, you're exhausted and feel emotionally put upon and drained.

Everywhere you look, the principle of the balance of give and receive is off in your life. You may also feel like you can't find your place or boss others around unconsciously trying to get them to take their place so that you can take yours and rest. You may struggle to find a place called home because *you* are not "home." Wherever lack of order exists and you have to get too big or too small, things just don't go right.

See how this "out of order" pattern spills over, making a mess of everything? Perhaps you are the epigenetic recipient of this pattern from some great-great-great-grandparent whose parents were drunken tavern-keepers, setting this pattern in motion back in Scotland 180 years ago! Your ancestor had to clean up their mess and run the show because his/her drunken parents couldn't manage. Now, all these generations later, it's up to you to change the pattern!

Unconscious Loyalties

You also want to understand something we call unconscious loyalties. Unsurprisingly, the most significant relationships we have are with our primary family members. Of that primary grouping, the most influential people in our lives are usually our parents.

Shining as positive examples as well as priming the pump for problems down the road, our parents are the ones we look to and model our lives upon as babies and little children, forming unconscious beliefs about how we're supposed to be and relate in the world.

Or perhaps it was an elder sibling who took up the parenting role and we look up to and pattern ourselves after them. Or we reject our parents and their patterns and end up running our lives in total opposition to them and we don't realize why. (We also don't realize that in rejecting our parents and how they are, acting out in opposition to them, is just as much a pattern of them controlling our lives as following in their footsteps would be.)

If a pattern we learn from a parent (or grandparent, or sibling, or any other admired family member) is a negative one, even when we know it's not good for us, we may emulate it out of unconscious loyalty, even to our detriment. Let's say you've picked up a parent's drinking problem. Because of unconscious loyalty to that person, it's hard to let the pattern go. The need to belong may also be in play. Or perhaps you don't want them to suffer alone, so you share the drinking problem with them. There are a number of observed patterns surrounding this.

Or perhaps the pattern in the family is to fail. Unconscious loyalties can then unconsciously prevent us from succeeding. Quite often I ask clients: "To whom are you loyal in the ways you suffer, struggle, fail, or even succeed?"

Bottom line, when under the influence of unconscious loyalties, we are in what's called a "systemic trance." We are quite literally hypnotized by our unconscious loyalty and can continue to run an unconscious loyalty pattern until it destroys us. On the flip side, it might drive us to change and make us into an amazing person.

Please note: In the drinking example above, the original pattern maker is quite likely driven by an unconscious, inherited pattern or excluded event that needs to change but is "stuck." Let's go back to the example of the perfectionist Army father figure. Let's say that rigid perfectionism doesn't work for his youngest daughter. She takes up alcohol as a way to escape the perfection pattern and a sense that she is failing and to avoid feeling guilty about rejecting the pattern and "Daddy."

Unfortunately, so often what begins as a solution (EG. avoiding pain) becomes a problem. The daughter basically starts a new pattern in the family system: Alcoholism as a way to avoid pain. Along comes *her* daughter who, through unconscious loyalty to *her* mom, emulates her drinking pattern. And so it goes.

Relational Patterns
Let's look at a few patterns that can develop and affect how we relate to ourselves and to others. Please remember that these are all patterns that are *unconsciously* passed down from generation to generation and they differ in language and content from person to person.

- **Repeating patterns and beliefs**

Sons often follow in Dad's footsteps regarding work ethic and how they relate to the world and relate to women. Daughters have a strong tendency to repeat their mothers' patterns in relationships. Paternal and maternal relating patterns can end up repeating for generations. This is why spousal abuse is a pattern that all too easily runs through a family line.

Or let's take the example of unfaithfulness. Maybe great-grandma's husband cheated and her mistrust of men becomes an emotional pattern of verbal expressions handed down from mother to daughter to granddaughter to great-granddaughter. Like, "All men are good for nothing." Or "Marry a man but never trust him."

Of course, maybe great-grandpa learned from *his* father that "Women will suffocate you boy. Don't let a wife trap you!" And that's why he cheated. And then *his* sons emulated their father and then so did the next generation of men and so on and on.

See how patterns of betrayal and mistrust can get passed down through both the matrilineal and patrilineal lines until they are seen and addressed?

- **Rejection**

The way we relate to men and the world around us, especially the business world, begins with our fathers. Rejecting the father figure for some reason, sons may struggle to find their masculinity or end up as overcompensating powerbrokers and tyrants. Daughters who reject their fathers may end up mistrusting men and much of the world itself. Or, again, through unconscious loyalty, they may end up dating a guy "just like dad" and then try to "fix" him in ways they couldn't fix dad.

Rejection of the mother can turn into a basic rejection of life, flow and birthing things (ideas, businesses etc.) or a refusal to be tender and nurturing to self, family and others. Rejection can express in a number of ways. Maybe Dad is distant and rarely home because he travels a lot for work. We end up feeling abandoned and reject his example, vowing to never be like that with our family. And then we become a helicopter parent, smothering our children with unwanted over-attention. Or, even though we reject a parent's relating style, because of unconscious loyalty we end up repeating the pattern. Our children may then also wind up rejecting us as they repeat the pattern.

- **Interrupted bonds**

When a parent leaves a young child for a period of time—even a few short days—this can create a jolt to the child's nervous system that expresses as a break in the bond of affection or an inability to trust this relationship and, by extension, often all others. The unconscious thought is: "I try and try and whenever I need someone, they are not there for me. Therefore, I do not trust relationships." Lo and behold, you end up in relationship with people you can't trust, over and over again. Each time as soon as commitment looms, the jolt to your nervous system stops it cold. And then the pattern repeats in the next generation and the next.

Creating strength and fulfillment in relationships

Every person in your life brings their system with them into the relationship. And you are a representative of your system! Creating strong, healthy relationships is very much a matter of understanding and dealing with your inherited emotional DNA patterns—and the inherited emotional DNA of the person standing in front of you, and then choosing to do some things differently ... hopefully to strengthen the system.

How do you do things differently? You acknowledge all that they are and all that they come from and all that you are and all that you came from and then make space for all that is possible through the two of you as mirrors of your individual family systems.

Everyone belongs in—and is the product of—multiple systems. Family systems, social systems, religious systems, economic systems, political systems. When we look at each other with inclusive eyes, hearts and minds, something entirely new is possible. Instead of repeating old dysfunctional relational patterns and passing them on, if we consciously deal with the patterns that are showing up and mine their gifts, we change and grow!

Strong and healthy relationships require intention, commitment and the desire and ability to build something together. Things like working on a project, creating a family, having joint accounts or building finances. Doing things together that carry the weight of creation in some way.

Listen to what you are telling yourself about others. Observe your patterns of relating. Compare that to the way your family system relates. Are there others who show the same pattern? What a great way to discover what's keeping you stuck as well as understanding the origin of your strengths in relationships.

By the end of this book, you will understand how to transform these stuck patterns, amplify your strengths, and vault ahead to a whole new way of relating with others and the world.

Health & Happiness Patterns

Just as we inherit relationship patterns, we inherit patterns of health and happiness. Having had your DNA analyzed, you know what your physical inheritance is—what diseases your body is predisposed to and what kind of exercise regime will work well for you. But remember, you also inherit emotional DNA—patterns of language, phrases, emotions, thoughts, beliefs, attitudes, actions, and inactions. And the emotional DNA patterns you inherit that affect your health and wellbeing are unique and specific only to you.

Sometimes specific health patterns are pretty wild, like my client who was terrified he was going to lose his right leg by the time he was 55. I've had any number of clients come to me saying their family was "cursed" with ill-health and other things, and Charlie was one of them. It took a while convincing him that the family "curse" was actually an *imprinted belief, cemented in place by fear, and passed down epigenetically from generation to generation, waiting for someone to see it and change it.*

I explained how a family system may have a belief pattern running through it that stems from a single powerful, event—like an ancestor losing a leg seven generations ago. The emotional DNA from that event is expressed very strongly in the thoughts, words, beliefs and fears of family members generation to generation, limiting and maybe even running their lives. Such was the case with Charlie.

Obtaining a broader view of his family's system dynamics and accepting the reality of epigenetically inherited emotions led to many personal insights and shifts that enabled him to release his fear that losing his leg was inevitable. By rewiring his brain and body, he broke the family pattern of fear around losing a leg and healed "the curse."

Happiness or a limited happiness quotient can also be inherited. I have had clients tell me they can't be too happy because disaster is likely right round the corner. We call this cherophobia. The question to ask here is: "What event in the past caused the restriction or limited definition of happiness to exist in this person?"

I have a client who wanted to be happy but who literally told me happiness was "not allowed." His father had fought in a war and came home with PTSD and deep survivor's guilt. He told all the children that they were not allowed to be happy. Other children had lost their fathers, soldiers he had killed on the field of battle. Although he survived, having taken the lives of others, he didn't feel like he or his children were entitled to be happy ever again.

- **Limiting health patterns**

When health patterns are passed down genetically and

epigenetically, there can be a sense of inevitability around contracting certain conditions. Yes, diseases can be inherited. But when we believe that to be inevitable, we close our eyes and hearts to what's possible and meekly repeat the prevailing patterns. We fail to see that medicine and lifestyles have changed and with it our own options and health possibilities.

We all know what hypochondria is—the excessive worry about one's health. And most of us probably know someone in the family who is always going to the doctor, worried excessively about their health. Something is always wrong. A flutter, an ache, a soreness, a cough—it's automatically cancer or something else that's incurable.

Hypochondria is frequently a symptom pointing towards a former family member who did not get the kind of medical help they needed in an emergency. Or they didn't receive the medical answers they needed to know at a time when they felt physically vulnerable—they never heard that their bodies were okay and that they were safe. They may have survived the episode, but the emotional "mark" left by not getting what was needed from a doctor can be seen in later generations whose members are chronically in search of healing answers.

This kind of worry pattern passed down through the generations limits the possibility of living a normal, exuberant, physically active life. It is important to also understand that systemically, hypochondria may stem from someone else's ill health or death that was not adequately explained, or even your own questions around an illness or condition that was never fully addressed.

Other family health patterns are more subtle. For example, the belief that "We're just not athletic people," or "Clumsiness runs in the family," or "We're just not the outdoors type," or "All the men die young in this family." These are limiting beliefs that can reduce one's ability to enjoy health and wellbeing in the body and promote a sense of fearful inevitability that then becomes a multigenerational truth.

- **Limiting happiness patterns**

A general sourness about life, an attitude of bleakness and negativity, a belief that "Nothing ever goes right," or "Nothing good ever happens to me"—all these kinds of thoughts and attitudes are emotional DNA patterns, unconsciously passed on from generation to generation. How many different "unhappiness" patterns can you think of that limit you and others around you? What family members are running such patterns? How about your friends?

How about the belief that the system always wins? Or that you'll never truly get ahead? How about, "I'm not good enough." Or "Nobody cares." Or "I can't____ (fill in the blank)." Or "I'm just unlucky," etc. etc.

We all know about this kind of limiting emotional DNA. These thoughts and attitudes are all around us—including in our family system and our social system. Being aware of these patterns and realizing they're often part of our emotional DNA inheritance is the start point to change these patterns. Understanding how they affect you comes first. Transforming them is the second part of the equation.

Of course, there are also the happy patterns that get passed on. Some people, no matter what's happening, are always smiling. Maybe that stems from a family belief such as, "You owe the world a smile" or "Life is beautiful" or "Things always works out." Even if you don't have the happiness pattern wired in, you can be the one to start it. Remember, as far as family inheritance is concerned, *you* are where it's at. Patterns can end—and start—with you.

Religious and spiritual patterns

This is in no way a critique or criticism of anyone's religion or spiritual beliefs. I'm simply going to point out that there are emotional DNA patterns—both healthy and unhealthy—that we all inherit from our family's and society's systems of religious and spiritual orientation.

Studies show that 70 percent of children raised in a religious family remain in that religion for the rest of their lives. Many beliefs we pick up are spiritually and morally uplifting, helping us to rise above our limitations. But there are other, not-so-uplifting beliefs, that we also inherit, such as the belief that life is about suffering. Or that suffering is the path to heaven. Or that humans are naturally sinful and deserve to suffer. Or that we are doomed by our karma to repeat unhealthy patterns and commit unloving acts. Or that God is constantly watching and judging us. Or that we will burn in hell for eternity for some sort of transgression. Or that money is evil.

Those are some heavy-hitting messages! The weight of the emotional patterns they can set in motion (and the meanings we make of them) can easily drag us down. And then those who come after us can get pulled into a downward spiral of guilt and depression as well. Even if you weren't raised in a religious family, take a look at where your ancestors came from and what *they* believed. Have you inherited old religious patterns of emotional DNA?

Business and Career Patterns

We often unconsciously migrate limiting or unresolved patterns from our personal relationships to our professional life and then wonder why we struggle with our careers. Peers may represent siblings. Authorities and seniors may represent parents—and limiting patterns can have us reacting to all of these people according to our own past experiences with the family members they remind us of, and/or our ancestors' experiences before us.

- **Family patterns in business**

One of the first things to do when contemplating issues in your career life is to look for repeating patterns from your family system. For example, maybe you're wondering why you chose your particular career or why you hang back in business meetings and don't easily share your ideas. You worry about being perceived as a "follower" and not a "go-getter" and don't know where to start to shift that.

You might ask yourself "When did this first start for me? What was happening in my life at the time? What did I make it mean and does anyone in my family line have a similar pattern?" Do you resist and resent authority? What was your relationship with your father/mother? What was their relationship like with *their* parents? Look for a repeating pattern.

Leaders and followers don't just happen. Who you are at home affects how you are at work. Later in this book you'll learn how to change that limiting pattern!

- **Transactional relationships**

Many business relationships are transactional. This is a known meta-pattern (a really big pattern shared by many). You give service and you receive compensation. You do X and somebody else agrees to do Y. These kinds of relationships are about getting what you need and giving what is needed for flow to happen. If you are interested in success, at the very least you strive to maintain a healthy balance of give and receive.

This is an ancient social, business, and economic pattern. It is not uplifting or transformative or philanthropic. It is also a pattern learned and passed down through family and business systems. "If you're good, then I'll give you a piece of candy." Or "If you're quiet, we'll go to the zoo later." Or "If you do that job well, you'll be recognized." Sound familiar? Meanwhile, the unconscious thoughts in your head as both a child and a business associate probably run something like: "Hmmm. Just how much do I have to do to be noticed and deemed a good child (or a good associate) and get that piece of candy/raise/bonus?"

In many transactional situations and relationships, there is a power struggle going on. And while transactional relationships get the job done, they don't get you promotions or recognition.

Transactional relationships can arise in any family or business system, but they are most notable in situations where they are unconsciously presented as a code of etiquette for the way to live and/or conduct business. No matter where and from whom you learn it, the transactional approach to life as "this is the way things are done" is obviously limiting and can cap your career. Once you accept it, the pattern repeats until someone questions the truth of it, and a new framework is formed. I'm sure you can see how restrictive this can be both personally and in your career.

- **Transformational relationships**

When we build relationships that engage higher emotional states than "What's in it for me?" magic happens. Higher emotional states can occur quite often in a family situation where the unconditional love pattern shows up, most often in the emotions of a parent for a child.

Unfortunately, unconditional love is easily lost underneath the weight of other patterns that run through families. Unconditional love often gets twisted up with patterns of guilt and sacrifice, for example, and then the love is no longer unconditional—although it is often confused and presented as such.

I'm not suggesting you try to bring something as powerful as unconditional love into the office on Monday morning! But there is a business version of that. *People don't buy products, they buy people.* And when people come together to accomplish something in a state of mutual curiosity and enthusiasm, kindness, and excitement, individual and collective potential can be tapped and harnessed. When these kinds of higher emotions are involved at work, there's far less competition and far more cooperation between people. Projects become win-win experiences. Work becomes a pleasure and even an adventure.

Even if you're the only person bringing this higher emotional content into the office or board meeting, it's still a win-win. Your work environment thrives, and *you* become a pleasure to work with. The end result is you become the person others seek out and want to invest time and money in. Advancement is a natural result.

Remember, your network is your net worth, whether in social terms, love and intimacy, or business.

When you genuinely show up, bringing higher emotions to the table—whether it's the kitchen table or the conference table—the playing field dramatically changes for the better for everyone.

- **Work as a J.O.B.**

Just like we inherit physical DNA, we inherit emotional DNA around our attitudes about work and career. Like any other systemic pattern, if we're not conscious of the inherited pattern, it can severely limit us.

For example, I once worked with an Army man who was up for promotion from major to colonel. Instead of being excited about his promotion, "Hank" was close to leaving the service altogether over the situation. Why? Because his father and his grandfather had both risen to the rank of major and gone no further. What made him think he deserved to be elevated above his forefathers? Major was good enough for them. It should be good enough for him!

I see this often in Genealogy 3.0 where children do not dare to do better than their parents for fear that doing so may hurt the parents. And yet a simple acknowledgement can make all the difference. A "Thanks Mom/Dad! Because of you I am doing well and getting ahead!" Remember, all systems want to evolve and grow. Your family system *needs* you to help it expand!

Or how about the blue-collar pattern? Or the Ph.D. pattern? "All my ancestors worked in this factory. I should aspire to nothing else." Or, "My whole family went to Harvard. QED I must go to Harvard." Or "Mom and Dad are both doctors, thus I should be a doctor." Some patterns are super helpful. The last two show a successful pattern buildout. But the "watchout" is to not become complacent and compromise your true self, but rather to elevate what has already been achieved.

Business/career, work patterns and money patterns all work together. Often the work pattern handed down to you is about how much money you're taught to believe you can earn. Or what kind of position you can aspire to. So many of us are taught that work is a slog and something you *have* to do. Not something you *want* to do. However, when you can plug into what you are doing with enthusiasm and joy, a plain old J.O.B can become an adventure. And that positively affects all the other areas of your life.

Pay attention to what you are called to do and ask where that came from and how you can incorporate it into your job. What were you taught as a child? What "family saying" or family attitude about money and work are you playing out? To whom are you unconsciously loyal in your career choice? What might happen if you moved beyond that loyalty and into passion?

Success/failure patterns
What is success? Ask ten people and you'll get ten different answers, all of which, no doubt, flow from their individual family's emotional DNA and ideas about success! However, because most of us are so heavily programmed by society's ideas of what success is, it's inevitable that most peoples' first thoughts involve money, mansions, sports cars, and prestige

But underneath family expectations and the social pressure, every person's definition of success is unique. For some, genuine success will entail acquiring safety, for another, health. For yet another, success will focus around creating a specific career. For another it will be about spiritual attainment. For someone else it will be about finding love and having a family.

No matter what "success" means to your family and to you, no matter how much it shows up, you can be sure it always comes loaded with a bunch of unresolved ancestral patterns around success or failure. How many stories have you read about people winning the lottery and then being in debt five years later? What about all the famous movie stars and rock stars—people at the pinnacle of outrageous fame and fortune—crashing and burning under the weight of drugs, porn and alcohol addiction?

How could that happen? Well, just as they had their own intentions (and yes, probably some family patterns) driving them towards success, they also had unexamined patterns that destroyed them—voices in their heads telling them, "You're not worthy of all this wealth!" or "Pride goes before fall, buddy!" or "Money is the playground of the devil. It'll ruin you!" or "Nothing good ever lasts." You know the voices I'm talking about.

Be aware that the little voices are often *multigenerational* voices and may not be your own inner voice at all.

Becoming aware of these kinds of influences and where they come from is the first step to their resolution and healing. The voices and the patterns—the successes and failures—all are clues to your own success and failure. Recognizing them, they become a great big bucketful of knobs and levers, doors and portals to possibility.

Remember, you have the ability to look beyond the multigenerational successes and failures and reach for your own success. The system wants that. It's how the world evolves. When people stretch and want and accomplish, *everybody* benefits.

Money Patterns
Money is not a commodity. It is a *relationship*—a relationship with flow and abundance, power and potential, creativity and imagination. It is also a wonderful friend, mentor and a disciplinarian. Unfortunately, given human history, it's can also be a rather scary relationship, riddled with issues, taboos and contradictions.

Since ancient times, we have worshipped and despised money, lusted after and rejected it, judged, misunderstand and misused it. Above all we have been taught to fear it and those who have it. A global force, money provides those who have it opportunities of every imaginable sort. For those who don't have it, money is an endless irritation and fearmonger that spells only limitation and failure. When our relationship with money is healthy, it supports us. When our relationship with money is tainted with greed, jealousy, hopelessness and despair, it just gives us more of the same.

Unless you were raised on a distant planet in another universe, you were raised in a family system and a national system on Earth that has developed its own unique relationship with money over the centuries. And you have inherited the patterns and bandwidths of that relationship. You've also undoubtedly created some emotional DNA of your own around money!

The easiest thing to do to figure out your emotional DNA around money is to look at your family and assess everybody's thoughts and attitudes about money, how much money they have or don't have, and how they act around money. Do your parents balance their bank accounts every month? Do they ignore them, hoping for the best? Do family members live on credit? Spend money the moment they get it? Never spend it if they can avoid it? Pinch every dime?

Now, see how well you and your relationship with money fit the family patterns. Examine your money language—the sayings you were raised with around money—the words you heard used to describe it, and the thoughts people expressed about it. What you, yourself, say and feel about it and the actions you take around it.

This is called "systemic language"—words, sentences, catch phrases, inside jokes, sayings—used around specific topics like money, sex, health, relationships, love, career, marriage, even life itself. Every family system has its own unique systemic language. (So do businesses and nations.) And, my, oh my, is a family's systemic language around money ever revealing!

Perhaps some of the following will sound familiar?
- We don't talk about money.
- It's not nice to talk about money.
- Only greedy people have money.
- It's not about the money.
- We don't need much.
- A fool and his money are soon parted.
- A penny saved is a penny earned.
- Love is more important than money.
- It's better to give than receive.
- A good name is better than riches
- I'd rather be happy then rich.
- Money can't buy love.
- You can have love or money but not both.

If you were raised hearing sentences like these (sentences that now populate your mind), how could you possibly have a thriving money attitude?

Systemic Sentences

As we have just seen, there are specific ways of talking about money and other hot topics in every family. Systemic sentences are like the air we breathe—we unconsciously absorb them growing up until the exact same words and phrases are running around inside our skulls, coloring everything. It doesn't take very long until we unconsciously come to believe that these sayings are the truth, when in fact it's just *our* truth. When that happens, the words become like gospel and we end up unconsciously living our lives by them.

Perhaps some of the following examples will sound familiar:
- Don't run with a stick, you'll poke your eye out.
- Familiarity breeds contempt.
- Hard work creates an honest man.
- You can't teach an old dog new tricks.
- Blood is thicker than water.
- You can't trust anyone over/under 30.
- You can't trust a _____. (Fill in the blank)

Systemic words and sentences were developed as part of your ancestors' direct reaction to those impactful events I talked about in the introduction—wars, famines, floods and various other disasters including economic crashes—events that ended up having life-altering emotional effects and thus became an inescapable, inheritable part of every family system. Do you know that much of Western systemic language around money results from the 1929 global economic crash and The Great Depression that followed?

The flip side is also true. Not everything said about money is negative. "Money makes the world go 'round" after all! Money is a wonderful facilitator of dreams, and how great is that? There is much to be said about talking nicely about money. And talking nicely *to* money. "I love money" is a great statement to make everyday. Quite frankly, I often tell money how helpful it is and how much I appreciate it. How much I enjoy having it around. After all, aren't those the kinds of things you would say to your friends? And wouldn't it be lovely to have money as your friend? And to have money as your friend YOU are going to have to rewire your brain and your epigenetic imprint. *You!*

As I've already discussed, whether positive or negative, the verbal patterns we adopt become mistaken for Truth (with a capital "T") and end up running our lives. That's great if they're positive. If negative, if we don't become aware of them and learn how to disentangle them and then transform our mindsets into more positive phraseology that can assist and uplift us on our life journey, they can definitely drag us down.

You want to build on all the successes, triumphs, and evolutions your family has experienced and change the negative impacts of the failures, miseries and stagnation. And your family system contains all the clues you need to break cycles of pain and create patterns of success.

And if you think you are exempt from ancestral family language because you were adopted or raised by wolves up near the Arctic Circle, sorry, it doesn't work that way. Even something as seemingly abstract as language is a pattern that gets stamped onto our genes.

I remember working with a radio show host who was adopted. When we got around to talking about systemic language, he laughed and said it was impossible that something like language could be inherited. Then he tracked down his birth parents and met them. And was he ever surprised!

"You won't believe it," he said in a session afterwards, "They have the same quirky way of talking that I do. My father has the same barking laugh. We even use some of the same weird Southern phrases, like 'If I had my druthers ...' Come on. My adoptive parents are New Yorkers and I've never lived in the South a day in my life. Even our hand gestures are the same!"

Moving On to Genealogy 2.0
So, now you know how to tell if you've inherited specific family patterns and if they're impacting your life. You also know some of the major patterns and the various areas of life they affect. In Part Two you're going to learn about Genealogy 2.0 and learn about the kinds of global events that imprint onto our DNA and trigger different kinds of emotional patterns in the first place.

EXERCISE:

Pick a personal issue you want to gain some insight into that falls into one of the pattern categories described in this chapter (relationship patterns, health & happiness patterns, business patterns, money patterns etc.) and let's get to work!
- What family members exhibit the same symptoms as you do around this issue?
- Are there family stories about ancestors that relate to where you feel stuck or strong?
- Can you relate the pattern to an impactful event in your family history?
- Is there systemic language in the family that relates to your issue?
- What question would prompt you to have one new thought, feeling and action? A thought, a feeling, an action that would start change happening?
- Ask "What's possible here?" Now, track what pops up for you!

PART II:

Genealogy 2.0

CHAPTER FOUR:

Meta-events and Meta-patterns

Now that you know you inherit patterns of thoughts, feelings, actions and inactions from your ancestors, patterns that affect every aspect of your life—relationships, success, money, health and happiness, etc.—I bet you're wondering, "Where and how did my ancestors pick up those patterns in the first place?" Great question!

All humans respond emotionally to their environment and the events that occur within it. When something happens—when there is an emergency, abuse, or some sort of upsetting event, or if a transformational situation occurs that has a strong enough impact—our individual emotional responses to the event affect our genes, laying down markers that affect gene expression in later generations. (If you need to go back and reread about epigenetics in chapter one, please do so.) A house fire, a divorce, a car crash, a shocking death, a sudden loss of income, a sudden promotion, or a sudden win are just a few examples of powerful personal events that change, not just our lives, but our genetics as well.

But it's not just personal events that trigger the creation of emotional DNA. Local, regional, national and global events are constantly affecting our bodies, our emotions, and our DNA. The bigger the event that occurs, the more our emotional response, the greater the epigenetic influence.

Let's take COVID as an example of a recent global event that is having tremendous emotional repercussions. It's too early to ascertain all the effects of the lockdowns and other mandates that were put in place in many countries during the years 2020-2021, but we already see a few trends.

Studies show a 22 percent drop in IQ in children born during the COVID years along[9] with an across-the-board increase in emotional and behavioral difficulties in children and young people.[10] The long-term use of masks has been shown to reduce emotion-recognition accuracy and perceived closeness between people.[11] Extreme polarization between vaccine proponents and any person voicing a concern about the vaccines has increased intolerance and group factionalism globally. Loss of jobs, income and family businesses were highly traumatic. The effects of the social distancing and widespread fear have yet to be determined.

On a more positive note, some people transformed their lives in amazing ways during those years, diving into projects and creative endeavors they always longed to explore but never had time to pursue. Many took positive control of their health. Some lost jobs they loved but others lost jobs they hated and ended up making positive career changes. Full time in-office work became temporarily obsolete and work-from-home opportunities exploded, positively affecting families and deepening emotional ties.

In constellations work, COVID is what is known as a meta-event: A major significant happening that *emotionally* impacts a wide number of people in any number of different ways. For example, year-long lockdowns may have triggered a sense of isolation and loneliness in one person that imprinted onto their DNA expression. Another person might have responded totally differently, using the solitary time for intense introspection and study—a journey that ended up being extremely healthy and growth-oriented. In yet another a drinking or drug pattern might well have been born. Or a combination of several different patterns might have been stimulated.

Every event offers an opportunity to struggle or thrive. There is no doubt that our descendants will be dealing with many difficult and limiting, as well as empowering and uplifting emotional DNA patterns for generations to come as a result of this global meta-event.

Different emotional DNA patterns can arise from the same event.

Because every human being responds differently to the same stimulus, different emotional patterns will arise from the same meta-event and be passed down to future generations. *The expression of inheritable emotional patterns is the direct result of how we individually choose to respond to a specific event.*

Let's use another major historical event—the September, 1498 earthquake in the Enshunada Sea, Japan, that triggered massive tsunamis along the coasts of Kii, Mikawa, Surugu, Izu and Sagami Bay—to see how this one event could have caused totally different kinds of epigenetic programs that were then passed down through the genetic lines of two different fishing families that were affected.

Here's how the first story goes: A family in Sagami Bay lost their only fishing boat, which sank, and their home was destroyed. The husband and elder son were lost at sea during the event. The mother, younger son and daughter watched the massive waves of the tsunami crash through their village from a high hill they managed to run to.

Both the son and daughter developed a hysterical fear of the water and refused to go near the sea ever again. The mother gave up all hope, fell into depression and she and her daughter became household slaves. The surviving son became an opium addict. Twenty-one generations later *you* come along with a fortunately mild, yet inexplicable case of hydrophobia and a glass-half-empty attitude about life.

Now, here's a different kind of response to the same meta-event. A fishing family on the coast of Mikawa Provence was also wiped out. The youngest son, the only family member who survived, responded by deciding to build his father's fishing business back up no matter what. With great determination the little boy went to work, eventually owning and running the biggest fishing fleet in Japan. Twenty-one generations later, *you* come along with a powerful "can do," glass-half-full attitude and become a successful entrepreneur.

See how this works? Granted science has yet to prove just how many generations emotional DNA can be transmitted. But again, because meta-events are so common from generation to generation, and emotional DNA patterns get triggered over and over again, it's not difficult to imagine how epigenetic influences could be transmitted from events occurring this far back in time, and even further.

Other meta-events
Let's take a quick look at other dramatic global meta-events that occurred over the last hundred years. How about the 2008 financial crisis? How about 9/11? World War II? The US attacks on Hiroshima and Nagasaki starting the Atomic Age, raising the specter of global nuclear war in the hearts and minds of billions? The Great Depression? World War I? All of these were, and still are, potent, emotion-stirring and emotion-shaping global meta-events.

Think about all the dangers experienced. The magnificent way people rose to meet difficulties. The acts of bravery. The miraculous rescues. Moments where people and whole nations came together for the greater good. The experiences, big and small, that occurred within those meta-events shape us to this day.

And it's not just global happenings that have an impact. Regional and local events do the same thing. For example, the current war in the Ukraine is having an enormous physical and emotional influence on the peoples of Eastern Europe and Russia. The Vietnam War didn't impact the whole world, but the populations of North and South Vietnam, Laos, Cambodia and the United States were deeply scarred by the 20-year conflict. In August 1931, the Yangtze River in China flooded, inundating more than 30,000 square miles, killing 3.7 million people, destroying over 40 million homes. All these large-scale, yet more localized disasters can be considered meta-events that end up leaving psychological and emotional scars.

Again, there are positive possibilities as well. Events like the 1893 Chicago World's Fair, famous for its "City of Light" display, changed the consciousness of the 27 million visitors who came away from the event knowing about AC power and how their lives would be changed by the application of electricity. Or how about the introduction of television in the 1950s and '60s, altering the face of communications and entertainment forever? Or the creation of Disneyland, the world's first fantasy theme park, uplifting the hearts and stimulating the imaginations of millions? And then Disney World, "the happiest place on earth."

Social events, such as the ratification of the 19th Amendment to the Constitution on August 18, 1920, guaranteeing women's right to vote in the US, and the same rights granted in the UK in 1928, uplifted an entire generation of women. An astounding meta-event that shifted sexual dynamics that had been locked in place for thousands of years, the passage of this legislation literally raised the self-esteem of women all around the world, imprinting their DNA with hope and a sense of greater self-esteem. The introduction of "the Pill" in 1960 was another far-reaching meta-event, freeing women from the fear of unwanted pregnancy, mitigating thousands of years of sexual fear and constraint.

The courage and inspiration of Martin Luther King Jr, and all the Civil Rights protestors in 1960s America sent a tsunami of positivity and empowerment into the hearts and minds of not just Black people the world over, but peoples of all races. When American astronaut Neil Armstrong stepped off the lunar landing module Eagle and became the first human to walk on the surface of the moon, July 20, 1969, an estimated 600 million people around the world were watching. The collective awe and excitement and hope generated that day was a meta-event of tremendous positive impact, imprinting the DNA of an entire generation with inspiration.

Can you think of other positive meta-events affecting us today?

Meta-patterns
Emotional patterns arise in response to meta-events, and they manifest across the full-spectrum of all possible emotional responses—joy, excitement, hope, determination, fear, depression,

anxiety, loneliness, OCD, paranoia, willingness, appreciation, inspiration, wonder, awe, you name it. In addition to typical individual emotions, as we saw above, there are also massive societal patterns that arise as *social* responses to events. These social patterns are called meta-patterns.

Meta-patterns generally develop across long periods of time as they are continually reinforced by social pressures and circumstances. But sometimes a powerful, quickly-established event, such as the advent of the Pill, can change the psyche and emotions of millions within a short space of time.

Now, let's take a look at some major global meta-patterns that most likely have affected your family system and are, as a result, possibly still affecting you.

The desire to belong

The desire to belong is one of the deepest, most profound of all meta-patterns found in all the peoples of Earth. It is a bone-deep need that drives much of humanity's choices and many of our personal choices, from choosing a partner and deciding to get married, to staying with a dysfunctional abusive partner, to joining a certain religion, choosing a political party, or signing up for a Yoga Mommas Meetup group.

Religion

Like most people, you might have been taught as a little kid not to bring up religion or politics in polite conversation. And there's a reason for this. Both are powerful ideologies that capture the mind and emotionally drive people, shaping an enormous part of their thinking and their beliefs, laying the foundation for how they live their lives.

Religious codes of conduct originally designed to guide, unite, and uplift humanity can be extremely positive. They can also end up as a bunch of rules and precepts that must be adhered to on pain of damnation and punishment. There's a big difference between the two religious commands "Thou shalt not kill" and "Kill the unbeliever!" One shows us how to live a more inclusive, harmonious existence. The other commands agreement and excludes those who do not follow the rules that have been established.

We may then see systems where membership arises through self-righteousness, division, prejudice, and fear, creating centuries of domination and subjugation. What was a solution in one era may prove to be an obstacle in subsequent ones if we don't explore, adapt and allow ourselves (and our beliefs!) to be flexible.

Here are few examples of meta-patterns inspired by religion both positive and negative.

Positive:
- Inspiration
- Group altruism and philanthropy
- Higher codes for living
- Commitment to a more loving and appreciative way of life
- Direction and purpose
- Community and mutual support
- Purpose

Negative:
- Lack of critical thinking
- Fanaticism
- Group mentality
- Messianic delusions
- A desperate need to believe in something as a crutch to avoid facing and resolving personal issues
- Punishment of any transgression

Nationalism

Pride of place. Pride of nation. Nationalism is a kind of belonging meta-pattern that can't help but rub off on all of us to some degree or another. Depending upon the amount of emotion behind it, belonging to a large national group is a meta-pattern that can give one a healthy sense of security, pride and safety. On the other hand, it can morph into an unhealthy fanatical adherence to a nation's beliefs, actions, and rules. "My country right or wrong!" And "You're either with us or against us."

An example of unhealthy nationalism was the fever that consumed Nazi Germany prior to and during World War II. In that case, nationalism—loyalty to one's country and one's leader—led millions of people to endorse and support genocide against Jews and Gypsies and other people not of pure Aryan blood.

On the other hand, the same time period and meta-event of World War II inspired incredible nationalism, grit, bravery, and determination in Great Britain and France as people endured and rose above Hitler's shadow to fight back. The profound nationalistic urge in America galvanized the equivalent of a new Industrial Revolution as researchers and scientists stepped up industrial production and women stepped into men's roles and went to work, lifting America into a position of being the greatest power on Earth.

Some symptoms of the nationalism meta-pattern are:

Positive:
- Pride
- A sense of belonging
- Unified effort and the cooperation in a common cause
- Standing as an example of higher possibility thinking and living

Negative:
- Fanatical thinking
- Us against them
- Exclusion of the rest of the world or specific countries
- Strong judgement against perceived "others"

Sexism, gender discrimination, and gender elevation
Gender roles and gender discrimination are excellent examples of meta-patterns. Sexual bias and sexual roles have an ancient history stretching back into prehistoric times when male/female roles developed strictly based on physical size and strength and the importance of child-bearing and safely raising children for survival of the species. Brawny men were the hunters and warriors. The more diminutive fertile females were relegated to more protected domestic tasks, including wild food gathering.

Neither role was considered better than the other, and the meta-pattern of equal but different gender roles was repeated and reinforced out of sheer practicality for millennia. And then the social *intention* behind the meta-pattern shifted. As civilization rose, wealth and property were accrued, and men began controlling the female body to ensure paternity for inheritance and succession. Women were still locked into domestic roles, but now it was for a completely different reason. And the "owned and controlled by men" status of women guaranteed that the domestic roles they played were subservient. Women and their work became diminished and less important than the dynamic, powerful roles the men played.

None of this shifted for thousands of years until widespread social and political changes, as well as technological development lifted much of the domestic burden from women, freeing up their time for other pursuits.

Eventually, the massive meta-event called World War II and the crying need for women to replace absent male workers in industry were major drivers for women's liberation in the 20th century.

Can you see that even apparently negative meta-events come with inherent gifts? Today, even the entire meta-pattern of gender itself—once believed to be strictly binary—is undergoing massive transformation!

Here are a few global symptoms revealing the current meta-patterns of gender bias and gender transformation:
- Increasing numbers of women in executive and leadership positions

- Increasing economic opportunities for women in second and third-world nations
- Feminine economy and the value of domestic work beginning to be recognized
- Greater caretaking of children being taken on by men
- Greater recognition of the rights of LGBTQIA individuals
- Women still paid less than men for the same job
- Women's values (love, cooperation, harmony, family, sustainability) are still often trumped by "masculine" values such as power, competition, control, independence, and limitless accrual of resources

Caste system
You don't have to live in India or have ancestors from those lineages to have inherited a sense of caste which is basically a meta-pattern of separation and superiority dividing peoples into different groups of social acceptability. Formalized and named in India, the meta-pattern of literally "casting" people into different social roles and holding them there is a global phenomenon as ancient as society itself.

    A free laborer is "better than" a servant. A merchant is better than a laborer. A land owner is better than a merchant. A local governor is better than a mere land owner. Of course, presidents, billionaires and royalty—lords and ladies, kings and queens—come out at the top of the caste heap as superior to everybody else lower on the pyramid. And yet, even as we look at the limiting symptoms of caste, we notice counterparts emerging as well. Common symptoms of the caste meta-pattern are:

    Positive:
- Determination
- Motivation
- Inspiration
- Being a change agent
- Pioneering spirit
- Creativity
- Imagination

Negative:
- Hopelessness and Worthlessness
- The delusion of "better than" and superiority
- "I can't"
- The system knows best
- Inability to take self-responsibility
- Inability to change– "I was born this way. This is who I am."

Racism

Racism occurs with the judgment of another ethnic group as "less than," justifying all sorts of acts and choices. Social devaluation moves towards marginalization that develops into segregation that results in all sorts of social and economic tyrannies, right on down to dehumanization and slavery. Patterns relating to racism can surface in both difficult and enabling ways.

Positive:
- Open-mindedness
- Rising up and supporting others
- Showcasing what others have to offer
- Community and connection
- Willingness to find how people are more alike instead of less alike
- Learning to look at capability rather than color

Negative:
- Self-righteousness
- Lack of critical thinking
- Mob mentality
- The "other" is dangerous or a negative influence and cannot belong
- Fear of contamination by the "other"

Victim and perpetrator
One of the most pervasive of all human meta-patterns is that of victim and perpetrator. This dynamic is the great human "sleep." Let's take the caste system and social marginalization as examples.

One might say that somebody born an "untouchable" is a victim of the social caste system, doomed to forever remain outside acceptable social norms. A child born in a ghetto in New York is also considered a victim of circumstances—subject to all sorts of inequitable situations such as a low standard of living, poor chances of accessing a good education and good health care, with little opportunity to rise above a situation which is seen as being perpetrated upon them by a rigid wealth system (caste again) that doesn't allow for upward mobility.

Here's how ingrained this meta-pattern is in the human psyche: All too often once those who have been victims rise in power and position, they turn around and become perpetrators themselves. The child born in the ghetto responds to the poverty pattern with outrage and violence, turns to a life of crime and ends up victimizing others. A whole nation of once-suppressed people kicks out those in power and then turns around and invests in revenge, marginalization and punishment of the very people who once dominated them. It's all very much a dynamic of "Wait 'til I get *my* turn on top, then you'll be sorry." Thus, the whole victim/perpetrator cycle simply continues.

Beyond victim/perpetrator, however, lies the potential for "Wait until it's *my* turn. I'll reach out to ALL people and show how we can all wake up and see how far we can go together." Some of the typical symptoms of this meta-pattern are:

Positive:
- Moving beyond prejudice
- Taking responsibility for my own advancement and progress
- Being a role model for unity
- Being a role model for love and kindness
- Self-respect and dignity

- Honor
- Prosperity

Negative:
- Sense of powerlessness
- "Poor me"
- Hatred and resentment of those perceived to have it better
- A desire for revenge upon the system (and individuals in the system)
- The system owes me
- "I'm going to just take what I can get"
- "I'll make them pay!"

War

War is a simply enormous meta-pattern that, to a great degree, arises out of all of the other above-mentioned meta-patterns, all of which are grounded in judgment, separation, inequality, fear, the need to survive or control, and the need to be better than others. *Globally, war is its own symptom.* But the meta-pattern of war has a number of survival patterns and symptoms that arise from being a soldier at war and/or being a civilian affected by the violence and destruction of war, such as:

Positive:
- Helping others in danger and need
- Kindness
- Courage
- Inspiration
- Technology
- Scientific collaboration
- Innovation
- Infrastructure rebuilding

Negative:
- PTSD
- Hypervigilance and continual processing. The brain,

and thus the body, are constantly in a state of hyper-attention, analysis and reaction, trying to discern what's safe and what's not
- Nightmares and insomnia
- Shame – the shame of having killed can be paralyzing, as well, it can create the subconscious need to in turn become a victim and suffer punishment
- Guilt – guilt over killing another
- Survivor's guilt often surfaces as an inability to thrive or live a normal life and can even result in suicide
- Domestic violence
- Inability to connect with others

As you can see, meta-patterns are the Big Guns, influencing nations, ethnicities, and cultures for hundreds of generations. Epigenetically, meta-patterns get passed down from generation to generation, creating mindsets that are the broad, sweeping shapers of whole societies. These ubiquitous patterns in turn affect smaller groups, trickling on down into family systems and individuals.

Each meta-pattern adds a layer of hypnotic imprints onto society. This is oftentimes experienced as a sense of inevitability, fate, or just "the way things are" here on planet Earth. Equally, each meta-pattern offers the potential for evolution, breakthroughs, miracles, and moments of powerful change for good. Which way we end up expressing a meta-pattern—positively or negatively—depends upon our inner exploration of our genealogy and its limitations and gifts.

Being caught in a meta-pattern places us into a kind of automatic thinking and decision-making mode called a *systemic trance*. However, its positive counterpart is the invitation to a larger adventure and a greater way of thinking and being.

Going along with the herd, accepting the unacceptable, perpetuating suffering and conflict, doing things "like they've always been done," happens when people are in a conditioned trance, locked into an invisible, self-perpetuating meta-pattern. However, once the pattern is seen for what it is, once the pattern is questioned, once a new way of thinking and being is desired, a new dream can be created. New, evolutionary ways of living can be developed and expressed and then those *new* patterns get passed on.

All it takes is one person wanting to experience life in a different way. Are you the pattern breaker in society and in your family line?

CHAPTER FIVE:

Linking Meta-events and Emotional DNA Patterns

Genealogy 2.0 is all about searching backwards in your genealogy chart to see if you can find any potential triggering events that might have occurred during any of your ancestors' lives, setting a particular limiting (or supportive!) pattern you're dealing with into motion.

Let's say you experience a consistent fear of failure (atychiphobia). It's there. You don't like it and want to shift out of it. First thing to do is check back through your own life to see if there are any possible triggering events that would result in this symptom. For example, perhaps a hypercritical teacher consistently humiliated you in fourth grade. Or maybe you forgot your lines on stage in front of hundreds of people during a community theater event and you felt you would die of embarrassment. Or even worse, there was that terrible moment when you failed to keep your baby sister from falling down the stairs and she broke her arm.

If there's nothing you can recall, the next thing to do is check out your family to see if anyone else is manifesting the same symptom(s) as you. If they are, chances are high you're dealing with a family pattern triggered by some personal family event or a meta-event in the past. (Or both!) In that case, use the information below to get a handle on what kind of event it was.

If nobody in your family seems to be dealing with what

you're dealing with, a meta-event in the past may still be the culprit. It can really help to check your family genealogy and see if there are any meta-events that occurred that relate to your issue. If, after you've done all that, your situation/symptoms are still puzzling and have no apparent cause, be assured you can still resolve it by going straight into the Genealogy 3.0 section and doing some of the exercises.

Specific meta-events
In this chapter we're going to look at different meta-events and the kinds of emotional DNA they might set into motion. Please note that this is not going to be a comprehensive listing of meta-events and their possible epigenetic impacts. That would take a book the size of an encyclopedia! But this listing will definitely give you an idea of the kind of events and the emotional ramifications you might be dealing with and evolving beyond.

Let's start by getting a handle on natural disasters in general. Living in physical bodies on a physical planet subject to meteor strikes, earthquakes, plate tectonics, volcanism, ice ages and sudden warming periods, tornedos, hurricanes, cyclones, tropical storms, floods, forest fires, and tsunamis implies a certain level of inherent risk just being here!

If we think of all the thousands of generations of ancestors that came before us who were subjected to all of those experiences since H. Sapiens lumbered onto the evolutionary stage some 200,000+ years ago, we get a pretty solid understanding of why our "flight, flight, and freeze" instincts are so well honed. We can also understand why fear/anxiety are so omnipresent in our species.

Of course, we modern-day folk have also inherited 200,000+ years' worth of emotional DNA influenced by idyllic moments dabbling our toes in fresh mountain streams, lying back and watching the clouds go by, holding our first-born child in our arms, making love for the first time, and sharing a wonderful dinner with family and friends—the grand yet simple things that make life worth living. And then there are the award-winning moments like successfully scaling Mount Everest or discovering a new way to help people heal from infections.

Bottom line, good or bad moments, we can't forget the past. It's still with us in our DNA. So, let's take a look at some of the meta-events across history that have helped shape humanity and the world we have today.

FLOODS

It's pretty obvious when I have a client who has a phobia around water that some event either in their lifetime or an ancestor's life may have set the fear pattern in motion. For example, one Chinese American woman I worked with who lived in the Southwest desert region of the US (quite deliberately) suffered from anxiety any time she traveled near water. The week her family spent visiting Disney World in Orlando, Florida was a traumatizing event that required anti-anxiety medication just to get her through it.

The phobia had been with her since she was a tiny child. When I asked her if any scary events had happened to her around water that she knew of, she said there was nothing. Which was why she was so puzzled. It wasn't until we looked back in her genealogy that we found the cause. Sure enough, her great-grandmother's family lost everything, including several family members, in the great 1887 flood of the Huang He River in China. It was the event that led her family to eventually emigrate to the US at the turn of the 19th century.

It's easy to trace an issue like hydrophobia to a traumatic event like that. But symptoms are often not that obvious. For example, one man I worked with came to me because he experienced consistent feelings of overwhelm, both at work and in his personal life.

Now, with some people it's very easy to determine the source of an issue because of the language they use. If someone came to me who constantly talked in water imagery—for example saying things like "My emotions just flood over me." Or "I feel like I'm going to be washed away by the events going on in my life," it wouldn't be long before I'd be asking them if they or their family had, at some time in history, gone through some sort of terrifying flood or tsunami event.

In this case, however, the man was simply chronically feeling overwhelmed and there were no language cues. However, when we dug back into family history, turns out his family had lived for generations on a farm near the Mississippi River in Louisiana—a location that was regularly flooded when the spring rains hit.

Cultures from all over the world have all sorts of myths and stories of a time of colossal flooding that may well have coincided with the end of the last Ice Age about 10,000 years ago. Geologists have discovered that, as the glaciers retreated, waters flooded from the Mediterranean Sea down into the area that is now the Black Sea, creating a waterfall 200 times the size of Niagara Falls! This deluge flooded vast amounts of what, at that time, was fertile farmland. The diaspora of fleeing farmers who were driven from their homes by the flood are believed to be the cause of the breakup of Indo-European languages and the source of the Biblical accounts of Noah and the flood.

India is home to several ancient tales of devastating floods sent by the gods to punish the unfaithful. The Aztec people of Mesoamerica reported a massive flood after which civilization had to start again. The scablands of western Washington State bear the scars of an unbelievably gigantic wall of water flooding the northwestern states. The creation of Hudson Bay and the Great Lakes are also the result of flooding and glacial melt. Locals in Normandy, France, still tell stories about the ancient days when people could walk to England. Instead of the current 22 kilometer-wide English Channel, there was only a large river to be crossed! The same kinds of stories abound throughout Indonesia. In ancient days, Australia was connected to the Asian land masses.

So, if you have any ancestors (and DNA) tracing back to North and South America, India, Indonesia, Australia, the Middle East, Britain and Europe, if you have any uncomfortable fears around water, or feel a need to run away in the face of looming natural disasters in search of better opportunities (and higher ground!); if you have consistent feelings of overwhelm and being "taken over" by life, this might be where and when the pattern started, many many generations ago.

The following is a brief listing of some of the worst floods and flood periods in the last 650 years. Obviously, if you're experiencing issues that might be related to these kinds of events, look back to your family's personal history and see how and where this dynamic may apply.

- January 1362 - The Saint Marcellus flood, aka the Grote Mandrenke (the Great Drowning of Men), was an intense storm that devastated the British Isles, the Netherlands, northern Germany, and Denmark, causing untold thousands of deaths. Historians note that sixty parishes in Denmark alone were "swallowed by the salt sea."
- January 30, 1607 - An enormous wave of seawater engulfed over 200 square miles of southwest England and Wales, completely submerging at least two dozen villages.
- 1560-today - Scientists have identified nine periods of major flooding in the European region, the most notable of which were western and central Europe between 1560-1580; almost all of Europe (1760-1800); western and southern Europe (1840-1870), and 1990-2016 (western and central Europe).
- 1841 - The entire Indus River Valley suffered one of the most damaging floods in recorded history.
- 1887 - The Yellow River (Huang He) in China flooded, covering 5,000 square miles of land and drowning up to two million people.
- August 1931- The Yangtze River flooded almost 70,000 square miles, killing as many as 3.7 million people.

TSUNAMIS

- 6000 BC - The Mount Etna debris avalanche plunged six cubic miles of dirt and rock into the Mediterranean Sea at more than 200 miles per hour creating a tsunami estimated to be 165 feet high, devastating Sicily and the coasts of Italy, Greece, Libya, Turkey and Egypt.
- 1600 BC - The eruption of the volcanic island of Thera in the Aegean caused massive tsunamis throughout the Mediterranean,

possibly triggering the end of the Minoan civilization.
- AD 551, an underwater earthquake unleashed a tsunami that flooded what is now Lebanon.
- September 1498 - Enshunada Sea, Japan – An earthquake, triggered a tsunami along the coasts of Kii, Mikawa, Surugu, Izu and Sagami.
- October 1707 - A magnitude 8.4 earthquake near Nankaido, Japan caused waves as high as 75 feet extending miles inland.
- November 1755 - A magnitude 8.5 earthquake near Lisbon, Portugal caused 90-foot waves to hit towns along the west coast of Portugal and southern Spain.
- Krakatau, Indonesia – 27 August 1883 - Waves over 100 feet high pummeled the shores of Sri Lanka and south India.
- December 2004 - A 9.1 magnitude earthquake off the coast of Sumatra, Indonesia created an 800-mile-long tsunami over 150 feet thigh that washed three miles inland, killing an estimated 227,898 people in 14 countries in one of the deadliest natural disasters in recorded history.
- March 2011 - A tsunami travelling 497 mph per hour with 30-foot-high waves hit the east coast of Japan, killing about 20,000 people.

Some Possible Emotional DNA Patterns Resulting from Floods & Tsunamis
What kind of emotional DNA patterns may be the result of an ancestor or ancestors experiencing such dramatic events?

Positive:
- Survivor skills
- Sustainability
- The ability to reinvent oneself
- Resilience
- Ability to always "keep one's head above water"
- Ability to "go with the flow"

Negative:
- Thalassaphobia (fear of large bodies of water)
- Hydrophobia (fear of water)
- OCD (fear of losing control)
- Hypervigilance
- PTSD
- Hoarding
- Sense of general overwhelm
- Fear of getting "swept away" by people, events, emotions etc.

EARTHQUAKES

Our bodies and minds are apt to translate things pretty literally. For example, if you or any of your earlier family members have been through a severe earthquake, going back to language again, your family (and you) might end up using words like, "I feel shaken to the core, " or "I feel like I can't get my feet on solid ground" or "I feel so unstable" or "I can't seem to find my feet." These are actually examples of what is called "system language" in systemic work and constellations. IE. the family system is passing along language that reflects that family system's life experiences of certain events.

- 526 AD - The Antioch earthquake hit the Byzantine Empire killing at least 250,000
- 1138 - Syrian city of Aleppo destroyed, killing around 230,000
- 1556 - Shaanxi Earthquake in China - 830,000 dead
- 1920 - Haiyun Earthquake (China 1920) - 240,000 dead
- 1976 - Tangshan earthquake, China, 242,000 dead
- 2004 - Indian Ocean Earthquake/Tsunami - 230,000 dead
- 2023 - Turkey - 7.8 and 7.3 magnitude - over 50,000 killed

Some Resulting Emotional DNA Patterns from Earthquakes

Positive:
- Resilience
- Agility
- Grit and determination
- Reinvention
- Balance
- The ability to create a sense of safety wherever you are
- Two feet firmly on the ground and being grounded

Negative:
- Claustrophobia
- Seismophobia
- PTSD
- Anxiety disorders
- A strong desire for safety above all else.
- A desire for stability (being on solid ground)

VOLCANIC ERUPTIONS

Remember the woman I talked about in chapter two who survived the violent eruption of the El Chichon volcano in Mexico? How she was always talking in terms of heat and explosives? Do you ever find yourself alluding to fire or heat? Do you suffer from an explosive temper or exhibit wildly kinetic behavior that resembles volcanic activity? Do friends sometimes describe you as being "off the charts?" Here are some historic examples of big volcanoes that affected lots of people.

• In 450 AD - Ilopango, El Salvador - The eruption of Ilopango is the second-biggest volcanic eruption in the last 200,000 years. Believed to have destroyed several Mayan cities and killed uncountable numbers of people, ash from the eruption darkened the skies around the world for more than a year, The eruption is believed to have caused the global cooling trend of AD 535-536, which led to famines and more loss of life across the globe.

- 79 AD - Mt Vesuvius, Italy - Ash and mud buried the nearby cities of Pompeii and Herculaneum killing 16,000 people.
- 1783 - Laki, Iceland - The Laki eruption lasted for eight months, emitting lava and toxic gases that poisoned crops and killed livestock, releasing enough sulfuric oxide to create global acid rain and drop global temperatures, causing famines in Iceland, Britain and as far away as Egypt.
- 1815 - Mt Tambora, Indonesia - The eruption killed up to 120,000 people.
- 1883 - Krakatoa, Indonesia - Waves over 100 feet high pummeled the shores of Sri Lanka and south India as a result of this event.
- 1902 - Mt Pelee, Caribbean - Destroyed the city of St Pierre, killing 28,000.
- 1991 - Mount Pinatubo, Philippines - The eruption ejected nearly 20 million tons of sulfur dioxide into the stratosphere, causing global temperatures to seriously drop.

Some Possible Resulting Emotional DNA Patterns from Volcanic Eruptions

Positive:
- The ability to run fast!
- Resilience
- Agility
- Grit and determination
- Reinvention
- Balance
- The ability to create a sense of safety wherever you are
- The ability to handle "heated" situations
- Two feet firmly on the ground and being grounded

Negative
- Seismophobia (fear of earthquakes)
- Pyrophobia (fear of fire)
- Tonitrophobia (fear of thunder)

- Phonophobia aka ligyrophobia or sonophobia (fear of loud noises)
- PTSD
- Anxiety disorders
- Respiratory issues
- Inflated language and feelings
- 'Burning desires'
- Hot language
- Caution around home locations

STORMS

I'm not going to try to list hurricanes, tornedoes and tropical storms which are all too common to get into. But, as you can imagine, experiencing disastrous storms may trigger many different kinds of emotional DNA patterns. You may find yourself wondering about your stormy relationships or questioning the storms within you.

Positive
- The ability to "remain calm during storms"
- The ability to "weather anything"
- Resilience
- Agility
- Reinvention
- Being the center of calm

Negative
- Ombrophobia (fear of rain)
- Strophobia (fear of storms)
- Tonitrophobia (fear of thunder)
- Phonophobia (fear of loud noises)
- Agoraphobia (fear of open outdoor spaces)
- PTSD
- Anxiety disorders
- Sense of defeat
- Fear of loss of "home"
- Hoarding

FAMINE

Are you hungry a lot of the time? Even though you're well fed? Are you hungry for information? Attention? Fame? Starving for affection? Can't stomach something or someone? Are you a hoarder?

Food shortages and famines have been around since time began. And they can't help but affect us mentally, emotionally, physically, and spiritually. The systemic symptoms of such as event can be obvious, such a chronic overeating. Or less obvious, like chronic overspending. Both are compensatory responses to an event like famine.

The following is but the tiniest sampling of famines that have struck every part of the world since 1250 BC. Many of these events were characterized by mass deaths, extreme levels of disease, and even, in the worst cases, infanticide and cannibalism.

- 1250 to 1100 B.C - Drought in Egypt
- 332 to 31 BC - Famine during the Ptolemaic Dynasty
- 400-500 AD - Western European famines help trigger the fall of the Roman Empire
- 499-502 AD - Famine in Northern Mesopotamia
- 927 - Byzantine Empire famine
- 1051 - Toltecs migrate to Mexico to escape famine
- 1230 - Kanki famine - worst in Japan's history
- 1315-1317 - The Great Famine of Europe east into Russia and south into Italy
- 1344 - India
- 1569-1598 - Various pan-European famines, Russia, Nordic countries
- 1601-1603 - Russia, Estonia
- 1649 - Northern England
- 1690-1700 - Scotland
- 1695-7 - Estonia and Sweden
- 1738-56 - West African famine
- 1740-41 - Irish famine

- 1810-49 - Four famine periods in China
- 1845-49 - Great Irish Famine
- 1876-79 - Famine hits Brazil, China, North Africa and India
- 1888-92 - Great Ethiopian Famine
- 1917-19 - Persian famine
- 1932-33 - Soviet Union (manmade famine caused by laws against crop farming)
- 1940-45 - Northern European, Germanic, Nordic famines from WWII
- 1945 - Vietnamese famine
- 1983-85 - Ethiopia
- 1994-98 - North Korean famine
- 2016-today - Yemen

Some Resulting Emotional DNA Patterns
It's not at all difficult to see the ripple effect of famine on humanity's emotional DNA.

Positive
- Making sure there's always enough
- Eye on the ball and trends mentality
- Accumulating wealth
- Healthy eating
- Food conservation and sustainability.
- Willingness to move as necessary
- Flexibility

Negative
- Eating disorders of all types
- Obesity
- Obsession with food
- Sense that there's never enough
- Unhealthy eating
- Hoarding
- Anxiety disorders
- Cibophobia (fear of eating or handling certain foods)

PLAGUES

Do you find yourself "plagued" by thoughts and/or ailments? Does the mere mention of the "flu season" send you running to the pharmacy for a flu shot? Or perhaps it sends you running for the hills instead, trying to avoid human contact? Are you morbidly curious about diseases? Hypochondriacal? Certain that the least ache or pain is cancer? The smallest sniffle COVID? Are you germophobic, buying hand sanitizer by the case lot? Do you fear getting sick? Dying?

Welcome to the club! We all know about plagues and pandemics first-hand nowadays. But humanity has always been subject to the ravages of strange diseases. And it has definitely affected our orientation towards both health and disease.

- 165-180 AD - The Antonine Plague is thought to have come from Roman soldiers returning from battle in the East. Over time, it spread throughout the Roman Empire and some of the tribes to the north. An estimated five million people were killed by the Antonine plague. During a second outbreak, a Roman historian named Dio Cassius wrote that 2,000 people were dying each day in Rome.
- 541–542 AD - The Plague of Justinian was a pandemic that afflicted the Eastern Roman Empire (Byzantine Empire), including its capital Constantinople.
- 541-750 AD - Various annual plagues throughout the Mediterranean and Europe thought to have killed over 100 million people.
- 1345-52 - The Black Death - Western Eurasia and North Africa - Thought to have killed upwards of 200 million people.
- 1492 - 1550 - "The Columbian Exchange" - The arrival of Europeans brought smallpox, measles and plague to the Caribbean and North and South American cultures, wiping out entire cultures. Uncounted millions died.
- 1817 - Cholera pandemic affecting Britain, Spain, Italy, Germany, Africa, Indonesia, China, Japan, and America.
- 1855 - The Third Plague - Bubonic plague in India and China claims over 16 million lives.

- 1918 - The Spanish Flu - Caused over 50 million deaths worldwide.
- 2020-2022 - SARS-coV-2 - Seven million deaths

Some Resulting Emotional DNA Patterns

Positive:
- Inventiveness
- Courage
- Compassion
- Caretaking of others
- Advances in medicine
- Determination to explore, identify and keep the future safe
- Immaculate hygiene

Negative
- Angry thoughts for or against vaccinations
- Germaphobia (fear of germs and microbes)
- Bacteriophobia
- Mysophobia (fear of dirt and germs
- Thanatophobia (fear of death)
- Hypochondria
- Nosophobia (fear of getting sick)
- Pathophobia (fear of disease)
- Algophobia (fear of pain)
- Aphenphosmophobia (fear of being touched
- Iatrophobia (fear of doctors)
- Hemophobia (fear of blood)
- Anxiety disorders
- Compulsive cleanliness
- Compulsive handwashing
- Necrophobia (fear of dead things
- Disconnection
- Mistrust of science
- Immersion in conspiracy theories

DIASPORAS

Before we leave this chapter, which is basically about the "cause and effects" of inherited emotional DNA, we need to take a look at the global phenomenon of diasporas.

The term comes from the Greek word meaning "to scatter about, disperse." It refers explicitly to a scattering of people across geographical space, time, and places—from nomads of northern Africa to the Tlingit peoples of the north.

The earliest Western studies of diasporas focused upon Jewish communities leaving the Palestine homeland starting around 586 BCE up through the first century AD, dispersing throughout most of what is now known as Eastern Europe, the Mediterranean coastal regions, Spain, and France.

Diasporas are most often the result of geographic upheavals, climate changes, famines, religious intolerance and wars. In more modern times, many peoples leave their homelands to pursue greater economic and job opportunities.

The diaspora experience itself is riddled with enormous emotional DNA-creating events both positive and negative. The wrenching emotional impact of leaving one's home and homeland, language, and all traditions behind cannot be underestimated. And then the flexibility needed to deal with all the complexities—class, race, language, local traditions, politics, religion, economics, immigration, and problems inherent in meeting up with "foreign" cultural influences and somehow moving into a different environment without losing one's original cultural and ethnic identity—is astoundingly courageous.

However, if this process is not undertaken consciously with gratitude and a conscious "goodbye" to the past and a grateful and accepting "hello" to the new, immigrants often find themselves unable to make the transition and wonder why they are unhappy, generally underperforming, uninspired, and feel like a fish out of water.

Do you feel a sense of displacement? Do you have the feeling you just don't belong? Are you restless, constantly trying to find the right "thing" so you can settle down? A house? A job? A lover or mate? Do you suffer from a feeling of rootlessness? The inability to commit? A chronic yearning for "greener pastures?" Are you sure that satisfaction, security, love and belonging lie just over the next hill?

Are you insecure? Do you feel subject to constant prejudice? Are you always checking around, seeing if you are fitting in? Do you constantly sublimate your own uniqueness in order to fit it?

These are a few commonplace systemic symptoms if you come from a lineage that has been on the move geographically. Yes, diasporas also trigger positive patterns, such as inspiration and the belief in opportunities for a new and better life. However, they are also one of the major ways that concentrated patterns inspired by specific events broaden in their genetic impact. For example, families leaving drought-struck regions subject to famine moving to more fertile climes will take with them the emotional DNA patterns initiated by famines and hunger, introducing that emotional DNA into a new geographic area.

Not surprisingly, diasporas are also frequently characterized by fierce clannishness, "purity" issues, deep longing, prejudice, and an almost desperate clinging to the concept of a lost mythical homeland. The struggle for authenticity and a stable identity for migrating peoples and their descendants can result in feeling lost. But it can also create the feeling of discovery, wonder, and finally a sense of being "found."

Some Resulting Emotional DNA Patterns from Diasporas

Positive:
- Pioneer syndrome
- The determination to do better
- The determination to represent one's old country well
- Expansiveness
- Gratitude for living in two cultures —in essence \ experiencing two lives in one lifetime

- A freedom to do things differently
- Flexibility
- Curiosity
- The ability to adapt
- Inclusivity and tolerance
- The ability to make things happen out of nothing
- The ability to start over and create success
- A global mindset

Negative:
- Inability to find a place or way to belong or fit in either at work or at home
- Anthropophobia (fear of others)
- Restless need to move and relocate continually
- Fear of persecution or exclusion
- Clannishness
- Refusal to change
- Clinging to the past
- Refusing to embrace the new
- Anxiety disorders
- Inexplicable underperformance – caught between the motherland and the new country

WARS

There is a lot to say about wars, especially with respect to Genealogy 3.0. War has its own system that is directly at odds with the norms of human behavior. Actions undertaken in battle go against all religious and ethical morality. They go against the heart and all common sense. There is not a human being alive on this planet whose emotional DNA is not influenced by the horrors of war or the innovations and the evolutionary jumps and emotional DNA distribution that it brings. Without noting the positive patterns along with the negative, we exclude the gifts it can bring, albeit in ways we do not like.

Some Resulting Emotional DNA Patterns from War

Positive
- Resilience
- Innovation
- Pioneer syndrome
- A need and passion for peace
- Inner peace
- Empathy
- Compassion
- An ability to understand multiple sides of an issue - mediation
- Inclusivity
- Being a peacemaker

Negative
- Anger
- Eye for an eye mentality
- Fear of violence
- Anxiety disorders
- Guilt
- Survivor's guilt
- Depression
- OCD

- Suicide
- Homelessness
- Isolation
- Anthropophobia (fear of others)
- Hypervigilance
- Necrophobia (fear of dead things)
- Hemophobia (fear of blood)
- Thanatophobia (fear of death)
- Phonophobia aka ligyrophobia or sonophobia (fear of loud noises)

Because war is still such a prevalent experience, I started to compile a list of wars between the year 1500 through the year 1989, just giving the date, name, years and link. And the list was 251 pages long! Far too long to include in this book. However, it is a simple matter to look up the listing of wars on Wikipedia by century, and then see what geographic locations were affected and when.

CHAPTER SIX:

Finding Meta-Event Locations

It's time to start linking meta-events to your personal genealogical information. The way to go about doing that is researching the different types of events that could have triggered your symptom(s)/issue(s), and seeing if any related meta-events occurred in the geographical areas revealed in your genealogical chart.

All the patterns and symptoms, positive and negative, we've covered in this section are part of Genealogy 2.0 and important to figuring out your personal issues and problems by relating them to certain events that may have occurred in your family history.

Connecting your symptoms and issues with possible past events in your genealogical history is a big undertaking and an even bigger opportunity to know more about what makes you tick. You can use the following listed Wikipedia links to view the locations and severity of meta-events around the globe for the past 500 years.

Please understand not every meta-event will be listed in Wikipedia. You may have to do some deeper digging using your specific genealogical information. Use the worksheets at the end of this section to take notes and enter information about your 1) issues/symptoms; 2) possible contributing meta-events 3) date and geographic genealogical matches.

In the next and final section, Genealogy 3.0, we address the issues and symptoms themselves, no matter where they came from, showing you how to address and transform your inherited

Emotional DNA and Emotional DNA patterns you're creating this lifetime, in ways that create happiness, increased security, better relationships, and success.

16th - 20th CENTURY EVENTS

Earthquakes
https://en.wikipedia.org/wiki/Category:16th-century_earthquakes
https://en.wikipedia.org/wiki/Category:17th-century_earthquakes
https://en.wikipedia.org/wiki/Category:18th-century_earthquakes
https://en.wikipedia.org/wiki/Category:19th-century_earthquakes
https://en.wikipedia.org/wiki/Category:20th-century_earthquakes

Volcanos
https://en.wikipedia.org/wiki/Category:16th-century_volcanic_events
https://en.wikipedia.org/wiki/Category:17th-century_volcanic_events
https://en.wikipedia.org/wiki/Category:18th-century_volcanic_events
https://en.wikipedia.org/wiki/Category:19th-century_volcanic_events
https://en.wikipedia.org/wiki/Category:20th-century_volcanic_events

Floods
https://en.wikipedia.org/wiki/Category:16th-century_floods
https://en.wikipedia.org/wiki/Category:17th-century_floods
https://en.wikipedia.org/wiki/Category:18th-century_floods
https://en.wikipedia.org/wiki/Category:19th-century_floods
https://en.wikipedia.org/wiki/Category:20th-century_floods

Famines
https://en.wikipedia.org/wiki/List_of_famines

Diasporas
https://en.wikipedia.org/wiki/List_of_diasporas

Wars
See Wikipedia

WORKSHEETS

ISSUE/SYMPTOMS	META EVENTS	DATE/LOCATION

ISSUE/SYMPTOMS	META EVENTS	DATE/LOCATION

ISSUE/SYMPTOMS	META EVENTS	DATE/LOCATION

PART III:

Genealogy 3.0

Transforming Your Emotional DNA Patterns

CHAPTER SEVEN:

Putting It All Together

So, here we are. You've had your genealogical chart done. You know the geographic areas where your ancestors lived. You know what meta-events have impacted those geographic locations. You know the types of Emotional DNA patterns that can arise from specific meta-events such as wars, volcanoes, fires and famines and have linked them to the personal issues you're dealing with.

Or perhaps nothing seems to ring any bells and still you're uncertain about meta-patterns that might be affecting you. That's okay. One thing you know for sure: You want to grow beyond limiting issues affecting you. Right? Showing you how to do just that—whether you can make a direct link to past ancestral events or not, is what this section is all about.

Dealing with inherited emotional DNA versus a new pattern
Whether emotional DNA patterns arising from meta-events live strongly in you or are barely noticeable, they're there. There isn't a person alive on this planet who has not inherited emotional DNA patterns from their ancestors. And, of course, each and every one of us are in the process of constantly creating our own emotional DNA patterns in response to the circumstances and events impacting our lives.

To be honest, issues are issues, no matter where and when and from whom they stem. However, one of the major positive effects of identifying ancestral Emotional DNA patterns is the fact that simply making the connection between a personal problem and ancestral patterns begins to shift the burden of thinking, "It's all my fault."

It immediately gets you out of wondering "Where the heck did my problem with _____ (fill in the blank) anxiety, shyness, addiction, overeating, etc., come from? What's wrong with me?" At the same time, please realize just because you can link a symptom to an event or meta-event in your ancestral past doesn't make it someone else's "fault" either. As you will see, the patterns are there for a reason, the most important of which is to get you to the next level of your life, whatever that is for you

If a new pattern is starting up with you—if you've recognized an event in your life that has set up a limiting pattern of thinking and/or behavior in you—you're also not at fault. Yes, it's sometimes hard not to jump on the "beat yourself up" bandwagon, because we humans are taught to blame ourselves and get down on ourselves for every little thing. (I think that must be an emotional DNA pattern that we both inherit AND create ourselves!)

The thing is, unless we live in a hermetically sealed basement and see no one and do nothing, life can't help but occasionally dish up events, people and circumstances that end up deeply impacting us emotionally. The question is, how do they affect us? Do we become the victims of circumstance? Or do we see events and their ramifications as opportunities for growth? How they affect us comes down to personal choice and action.

There is no "scale of impact"
As I've said before, the more powerful the event and the emotions involved, the greater the impact on our DNA. Remember the woman I talked about in chapter two who survived the violent eruption of the El Chichon volcano when she was a little girl? How she was always running, on the go, exaggerating everything, using fire terms in her speech all the time? It was not her fault that this happened and that she was affected by the event this way. But she has some unique opportunities in terms of how she continues to be affected by

the event and how she can use it to thrive. The same is true for you.

Whether it's a volcano or a car crash, a bad romantic breakup or losing your 401K, there's no "scale of impact," no rule written somewhere that says that X event will impact people to Y degree and no more.

For some people losing their job can be the equivalent of a volcanic event. Being yelled at for leaving your toys all over the living room rug can be devastating. Everybody is unique in their sensitivities and meaning making.

You can't compare yourself and your emotional reactions to anybody else.

You can't blame yourself for picking up emotional triggers, issues, blocks, misperceptions and limitations. It's just part of life. But you can do something about them and with them! In fact, they are your clues to moving out of stuckness and into a remarkable life.

So, are you ready to get some transformation happening? Ready to embrace change? Great! Here are the twelve steps. Ready?

THE TWELVE STEPS

STEP ONE:
Choose the issue/pattern you want to address

First thing to do is determine what pattern you want to evolve and transform. If you're uncertain ask yourself:
- Where do I feel the most unhappy and stuck?
- What is absolutely not working for me right now?

Stuck in a job going nowhere? Or maybe you're in an unhealthy relationship? Or perhaps you're dealing with chronic anxiety?

Whatever is the most "up" for you is where you want to start exploring.
- Start by noticing your thoughts, feelings, and actions around this issue
- Don't pick an issue you think you *should* shift. Pick the issue your heart wants to see transcended. The issue your gut is tired of holding in a tight knot and your brain is tired over overthinking.
- Don't sanitize it. Don't try to make it look or sound pretty.

Your issue is exactly the way it is for a very good reason. It's speaking directly to you the way you would understand it.

**If you do not acknowledge that
your issue exists exactly the way it is,
you won't be able to shift it.**

In systemic work we call this "acknowledging what is." Only when you do this can you start looking at where you want to shift.

STEP TWO:
Create your statement of acknowledgement

As you notice your thoughts, feelings and actions around this issue simply go to your bottom line or core. What do you want to say about this? Sometimes just this identifying action can create large shifts.

Create a simple sentence that summarizes and embodies your problem/issue clearly and simply.

Examples:
- I feel stuck.

- I'm afraid of losing everything.
- I'm afraid of standing out.
- I'm exhausted and overwhelmed—by life, work, people, everything.

STEP THREE:
Is this a family pattern?

1) Determine if anyone in your family system seems to be dealing with (or has ever dealt with) the same issue you've chosen (or a nuance and flavor of it) either directly or in some tangential sort of way. Notice the language and actions that seem to recur. Look for odd reactions to this issue, like heightened fear, anger, stubbornness. If they're present, you know you're dealing with a family pattern.

2) If this is a noticeable family pattern, see if you can trace it back through your family lineage and find potential triggering meta-events that might have set this pattern in motion.

3) If this is NOT a noticeable family pattern in others, still see if you can trace it back through your family lineage and find potential triggering meta-events setting this pattern in motion.

4) If you find no events and this is not a family pattern, this could be YOU in the process of developing a pattern. Look back into your life and see what events might have triggered a strong emotional reaction that might be driving the problem you're facing.

STEP FOUR:
Activate your body compass

You might not have realized it, but your body is a kind of "truth telling" device. Ever had a feeling that something was off? That some person or some situation just felt "wrong?" Maybe you're interviewing for a broker job and everything the money manager is saying sounds perfect. The promised pay is fantastic. But something just doesn't feel right. There's no logic to it, but despite everything you decide not to take the job. Then, six months later, you hear the firm was busted for insider trading and all the mid-level traders (of which you would have been one) got investigated and now have black marks on their resumes.

Some call this "following your gut" or "following your heart." And for good reason! Science has proven that both the heart and the gut have neurons just like in your brain. Both the heart and gut act as a neuron plexus or "alternative brain" to your system.

Bottom line, the body doesn't lie. It doesn't know how to lie. Your brain, heart and gut are your three best guides in life. Good businessmen understand this quite well. You can feel when your body knows something isn't good for it (and you). Some people call this intuition, but it's actually you paying attention to this potent threesome that is constantly trying to give you clues. Either way, it pays to learn how to tune into this truth-telling device so you can use it wisely.

STEP FIVE:
Apply your body compass to your issue

1) Write down your issue on a large piece of paper. Let's say it's dealing with lack and money issues. Notice your thoughts, feelings, and actions as you write.

2) Decide, "What do I want most? What do I yearn to experience instead of lack?"

3) Write your answer down on another piece of paper. For example, write SIX-FIGURE INCOME on that piece of paper.
4) Place both pieces of paper on the floor as far apart as you can manage. Stand between the two pieces of paper and listen for the

voices that start to pop up. What are they saying? (By the way, please note that these voices are frequently the voices of your ancestors. All the things they said to themselves and others, echoing down to you as clues.)

5) Tune into what you feel about the two pieces of paper and their two different messages. Which way are you pulled? Often when you're pulled towards the issue, this may indicate a multigenerational pattern with a strong voice. When you are pulled towards your dream, either that is an unrecognized multigenerational pattern showing up that allows and supports dreaming, or you are creating a pull that is stronger than what has you stuck. And THAT is what you want to achieve.

Your dream *has* to be stronger than your current state of being or you won't move.

6) Step closer towards your desire. How does your body feel as you get nearer to your dream? Excited? Notice where you feel the excitement in your body. Scared? Notice where that is.

7) Now move the other way, back towards your issue of lack. How does your body feel? Is there a sinking sensation? Sorrow? Heaviness? Relief? Note everything you feel and where you feel it in your body.

8) Now move back towards your desire of a six-figure income and repeat the process.

9) If you find yourself feeling happier, lighter, freer, excited, filled with gratitude etc. as you move towards your dream, you KNOW you're on the right track, pointed in the right direction with your desire. You're moving beyond the trance of the old multigenerational pattern that has held you in its grip.

10) If something comes up—if you get a flash of a step you can take that will facilitate your dream, stop and write it down and place that new piece of paper on the floor closer to your dream than mid-point.

11) Stand on that step. How does that step feel? Where do you feel it? Does another step occur to you? Write it down and place the next piece of paper closer towards your goal and go stand there. How does *that* feel? Etc.

STEP SIX:
Imagine your new life

Ask yourself this very important question: "What would my life be like if I really went for my dream?" Seriously, take a good amount of time to examine this question. Play with the idea. Imagine what your life will be like, earning over $100K a year.
- Are there added responsibilities?
- Do you feel a surge of self-worth?
- Are there limitations?
- Are new adventures popping into your brain that money will facilitate?
- Do you feel guilt around earning more?
- Do you feel more safe and secure?

This process is how you tune into your inner compass. You know what you don't want, and you know what you do want. You've paid conscious attention to your body's feelings ... its compass around the issue. Now you're ready to go to the next step.

STEP SEVEN:
Create a personal constellation (this is you playing in 3D)

Remember the story of Terry and her missing grandmother in Chapter One? How she discovered the answer to her life-long puzzling sense of isolation by creating a family constellation and walking through it? Well, you're going to create one right now!

Doing a constellation will not only enable you to get more personal insights and resolution around your issue, doing a constellation in 3D and walking through it, seeing things from a totally new perspective, will literally rewire your brain in present time. How? Because when you see a relationship dynamic for the very first time, the AHA! shifts the neurons in your brain into a whole new pattern in mere seconds.

Remember, a constellation is a physical representation of your family and issue. Here's the graphic image we saw earlier.

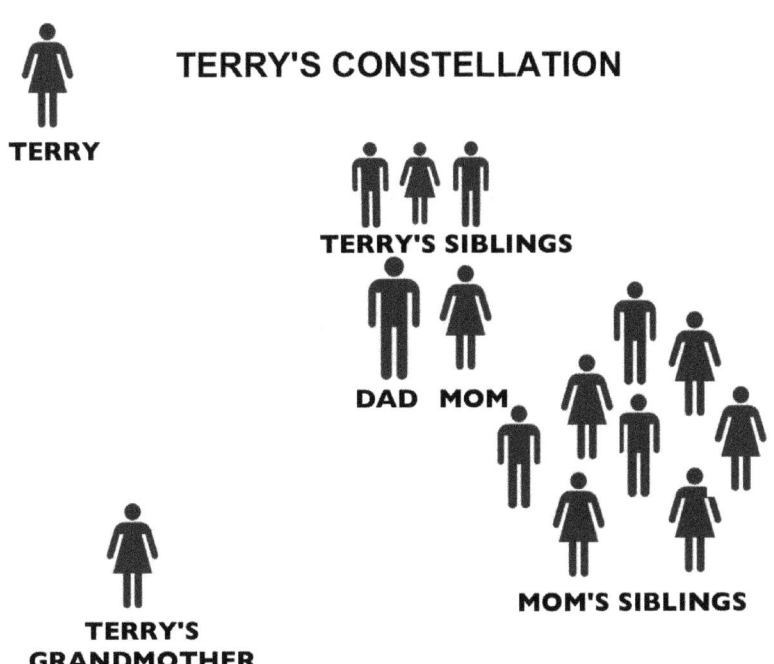

1) If you can connect your issue to your family, and if you happen to have enough people hanging around with nothing else to do and a big enough empty space to do it in, you could create a constellation with human representatives. However, for most people this just isn't practical. (Plus, your friends might think it's too weird—until, that is, they see the information surfacing in front of them at which point be prepared to do a whole bunch of constellations!)

If no one is available, use individual pieces of paper for each family member "Mom," "Dad," sister's name(s), brother's name(s), etc. Or use whatever else you've got handy—objects, chess pieces, figurines, etc.)

Arrange the constellation in a way that feels/seems right to you as far as the relationships between family members are concerned.

- Don't forget to place yourself in the constellation!
- Make sure your issue is represented on a piece of paper as well.

Remember, the whole point of a constellation is using it to create dimensionality, to bring your issue to life by bringing all your senses into play. You want to have an embodied experience of the situation, engaging multiple senses so that your body, brain and mind can process and rewire your new thoughts, feelings and actions. So, it's best to lay your constellation out on the floor in a big room, or on a patio or on the lawn.

(If you only have a small space to do this, use Post-Its on a tabletop.)

Now, stand on (or next) to the paper representing you.
- Look around. Notice who is close together and who is far apart.
- Notice the pattern of family members around you.
- Is everybody where they should be?
- If something feels off, rearrange until it feels right.

- Take your time.
- Be open to any insights that might arise as you're doing this.
- Do you notice a pattern or a relationship dynamic that relates to your issue that might help explain your issue?

Walk through the constellation. Notice how your body feels. Notice any thoughts, ideas, impressions that come up around your family, yourself, and your issue. It might help to carry your phone with you and record your impressions as you do this.

- Take a break and write down any insights you had.
- Note what you're feeling.

Do you feel a sense of relief? Anxiety? Overwhelm? Anger?

2) If you haven't been able to connect your issue to your family, create a constellation specifically around your issue addressing such things as:
- When the issue first started.
- What was the initiating event?
- Your feelings about the issue
- Triggers that stimulate the issue, making it worse
- Mitigators that soothe the issue, making it less prevalent

Here is an example of what that might look like. (The grey blocks represent pieces of paper on the floor or tabletop.)

ISSUE CONSTELLATION ON LACK/SCARCITY

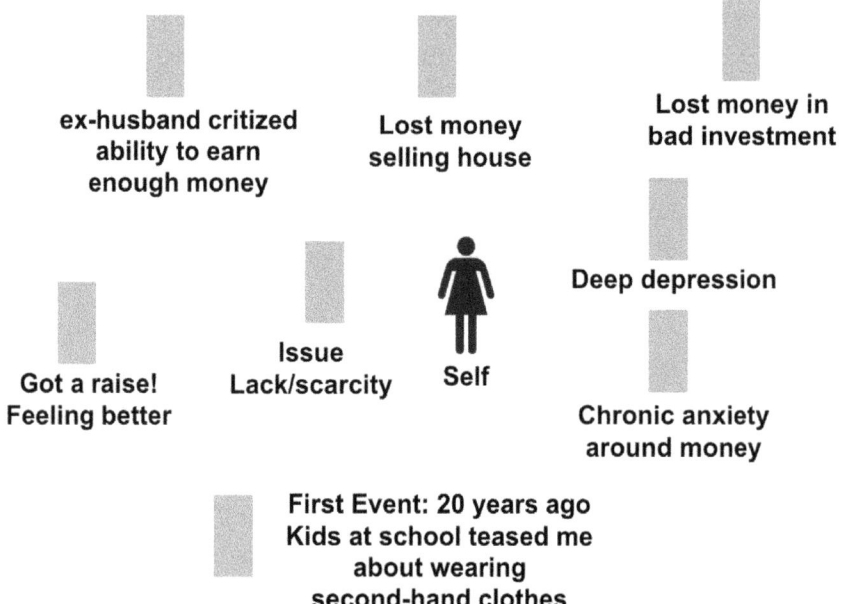

Stand on (or next) to the paper representing you.
- Look around. Notice what experiences are close to you and which are farther away.
- Notice the pattern of events around you.
- Is everything where it should be?
- If something feels off, rearrange until the pattern seems right.
- Take your time.
- Be open to any insights that might arise as you're doing this.

Walk through the constellation. Notice how your body feels. Notice any thoughts, ideas, impressions that come up around yourself, and your issue. It might help to carry your phone with you and record your impressions as you do this.

Take a break and write down any insights you had. Note what

you're feeling. Do you feel a sense of relief? Anxiety? Overwhelm? Anger? Fear? Frustration? Hopelessness? Etc.

Take the time to let the feelings and insights sink in.

STEP EIGHT:
Acknowledging inherited ancestral patterns

If you found meta-events in your ancestral history that would explain an issue around lack and not earning over a certain amount of money (or whatever issue you're working on), now is the time to contemplate that influence. Maybe your great-great-grandparents were poor immigrants. Maybe your great-great-great-great-great-grandparents were indentured servants. Maybe they were slaves. Maybe you had ancestors who fled from a war zone with nothing but the clothes on their backs. Maybe an ancestor was very rich and lost it all.

Think about your ancestor(s) who experienced this trauma event. Acknowledge them and acknowledge what happened. Acknowledge the epigenetic ripple effect that brought this pattern to you. Acknowledge that the pattern is NOT YOU and that you are in no way at fault. Realize:

- Everybody did the best they could.
- You have done your best as well.
- Fault and blame serve no one.
- **Where you are now is no indicator of where you can end up.**

Breathe that in and sit with it for a moment!

STEP NINE:
Find the gift and your own new contribution

This is such an important step! I know it might seem weird or even impossible to "find the gift" in a pattern that has limited and distressed you and caused you pain. However, it has served a purpose by getting you to this point. Being able to see that is a huge step towards healing and transformation.

Let me give you an example. Danielle's mom left her and her father when she was six years old. To say she had abandonment issues and difficulty trusting people would be an understatement. And yet when I asked her to find the gift in the situation, she realized her mother leaving had not only given her great strength and resilience, it had also cracked her heart open and given her the fierce resolve to care for others in ways she hadn't experienced.

Many times, healing lies in doing for others what we wish had been done for us. We get to go through the experience differently. Doing this work also gave her the insight that she was loyal to a fault with her friends. She realized she had to learn to take care of herself as well.

It's not always easy to find the gift in a difficult family pattern. But it's always there. And if you're struggling with the pattern of abuse and find it hard to forgive abuse that has occurred, remember this is a pattern that has been passed down. Others in your family may be victims of a similar pattern, but this is about you finding a new path and a bigger life. Acknowledging what we have gained through pain and difficulty or joy and gratitude is a big step on the path forward.

STEP TEN:
Create your sentence of resolution

You have your acknowledgment statement. Now it's time to create the statement that epitomizes your commitment to end the situation.

Let's say your acknowledging statement is something like: "I am stuck in a lack mindset that limits my income." A statement of resolution could be something like:
- I'm done with not making enough money!
- This doesn't belong to me. It's time for me to change
- I no longer need to keep settling for a low income!
- My money pattern of lack stops now!
- I am no longer the victim of lack/scarcity thinking!

STEP ELEVEN:
Create your sentence of re-solution

This is your "and then what?" statement. It firmly places your feet on the path to growth and transformation. As opposed to the statement of resolution, which is about completing the past, your statement of re-solution is a declaration of your future. This is not some airy-fairy pie-in-the-sky idea.

This is you rewiring your brain.

You've acknowledged you're done with not making enough money ... now what? What's possible right now? What would be a really good outcome if this were to change? The following are realistic yet empowering answers to those questions:
- I am teaching myself to receive an abundance of money and good things in my life.
- I am valuable and continue to build my value and I receive accordingly.
- My sense of self-worth, excitement, and determination increase daily.
- As my income increases, I am both wise and generous with my money. Money and I are friends.

Don't go all "pie in the sky" crazy with your sentence of re-solution. Your brain has to give your body a story it can believe. I can't state that enough, If you get too "out there," you won't believe your new goal is really possible. And if your mind and body don't both believe something is possible, it's not going to happen.

At the same time make your statement emotionally powerful. You want to FEEL inspired by your statement of re-solution. Elevated emotions like excitement, joy, enthusiasm, determination are the juice that will get you all the way to your goal.

STEP TWELVE: |
Set goals and don't stop.

Sit down and decide what steps you can take to walk into your new life. Is it looking for a new job? Finding out about investment strategies? Take small steps. Maybe you need to rework your resume or find an accountant. Or go and invest in something that makes you feel good—and abundant!

There are no rules about the goal setting process except set some goals and take steps—no matter how big or small—towards your dream.

Don't stop setting goals! The minute you achieve one, set the next. Keep going! And be sure to celebrate each time you achieve a goal. Acknowledge yourself and do something nice for yourself. This is part of investing in your own adventure. And just think, not only are you doing things for yourself that expand you and make you happy, you're setting new positive patterns into motion for your descendants to enjoy and appreciate!

CHAPTER EIGHT:

You Are The Game Changer

Amazing positive change is not in a galaxy far, far away. Healing limiting family/ancestral patterns isn't a pipe dream. A better life, more satisfying relationships, more money, abundance and security don't happen to just the lucky few in this world. When you have the desire, the right tools, and apply elevated emotions and a "go to" attitude, it's possible to achieve all of that, starting right from where you're currently "at." (Where else can you start from?)

The Systemic Work & Constellations tools I've given you in this book, when applied to the information available to you through your genealogical chart, can work magic in your life if you apply them. There is not a single issue a human being faces—sexual abuse, trauma of every nature, health problems, emotional dysfunction—that doing the work outlined here can't help. And I should know. I've worked with thousands of people over the years, helping them get out of dysfunctional family patterns, deal with unfinished issues, and get on with living the kind of lives they'd always dreamed of living.

But before we close, I'd like to talk about a couple more things.

Elevated emotions
In chapter three, I briefly mentioned the value of expressing higher emotions—emotions like happiness, contentment, appreciation, hope, compassion, understanding, gratitude, and yes, love. I'd like

to zero in on the topic of higher emotions and explain a little of what they can do for you.

When we're stuck in old, limiting family patterns, the very fact that they're limiting means they carry with them lower emotions and stressed states of mind. Nobody thrives amidst tired old patterns of thought and action. Boredom, criticism, depression, anxiety, a sense of repetition and hopelessness ... if you're experiencing any of these kinds of "drag-me-down" emotions, it's highly likely you're unconsciously caught in an ancestral pattern.

The very fact that you're reading these words means you're already elevating yourself beyond that pattern.

You're looking for change. You desire it. And desire is a tremendously positive, powerful emotion. Possibility is a close companion. When you desire change and just a little bit of possibility walks in the door, you're already operating at a higher frequency level than you were, caught in a limiting ancestral pattern. You're already lifting yourself up by your emotional bootstraps.

Determination is another powerful emotion. If you discover epigenetic patterns slowing you down and keeping you stuck, and you approach the exercises in this book with the determination to make change happen—and then you follow the above 12 steps—change WILL happen.

Commitment is another high-level emotion and mindset that keeps you dialed into the adventure from start to finish. When my clients definitively tell me: "I am doing_X_," they have no excuses. They have determined where they are going and what they need to do to get there. They have made a choice, locked it in, and are not open to reasons why they can't get the job done.

Sure, the old voices saying "you can't ..." might still be hanging around. But if you know where those limiting voices are coming from ... if you know those voices don't really belong to you ... if you know those lingering thoughts are just a habit, you can put those voices in their rightful place where they will quickly become smaller and quieter until they disappear altogether.

So, what do I mean by commitment? Commitment means you don't quit after a day, a week or even a year. You stay the course even when you are tired and want to give up. You know what you want, and you simply keep on going towards that goal. And know this: No step towards your goal is too small! As long as you're moving forward, you're moving forward. Don't judge the size of the step. (Lower-order emotion.) Congratulate yourself on taking the step. Celebrate! (Higher-order emotions.)

As you follow the steps outlined in the previous chapter and you start getting insights into your issues, excitement will start to show up and build. And once you hit the excitement stage, you've really created momentum.

So, why do elevated emotions make such a difference? Well, have you ever had one of those days when you woke up happy for no reason and everything just seemed to go right that day? On the flip side, have you ever gotten up on the "wrong side of the bed?" And then everything just went from bad to worse (including your mood) the whole day long? What you've experienced in both cases was the result of the mindset your emotions were emanating. The "vibe" if you will.

Being happy for no reason quite literally aligned you with situations, people, and circumstances that matched "happy." Being grouchy for no reason quite literally magnetized lower frequency situations, people, and circumstances to you that matched "grouchy."

The thoughts and emotions you generate
draw matching circumstances to you.
That's the way life works.

Elevated emotions help us to put down old wounds, tired assumptions, and repetitive patterns, opening our heart, mind, and gut to new possibilities and potentials. Exuding a sense of enthusiasm and excitement brings us an entirely different outcome than the thoughts and emotions that got us—and our ancestors—stuck in the first place. When you're excited and enthusiastic, your brain literally initiates the production of "happy-making" biochemicals like dopamine that make you feel even more positive. And your physical body responds with increased health and wellbeing when it isn't being bombarded with the stress hormones triggered by lower emotions.

    Can you see the upward spiraling positive impact? This is what you want to set into motion: Higher emotions creating circumstance that create higher emotions. Then you're well on your way.

Supporting the creation of elevated emotions
When you get to Step Six (as outlined in the previous chapter) make sure that when you imagine your new life that you don't set yourself up by creating a dream you won't really be able to believe in and get behind. For example, dreaming about becoming a millionaire in a year's time. It's certainly not impossible. But in your heart of hearts do you believe you can do it?

    This is the key question to ask yourself while on Step Six. If the honest answer is, "no," what emotion(s) will you be embodying as you go about doing the work to attain that particular dream? Doubt. Disbelief. Uncertainty. Distrust. Fear of failure. All of which are lower emotions—emotions that will be sabotaging you every step of the way.

    So, be sure to dream a dream that you can believe in! Like becoming a millionaire with no time period attached to it. Can you get behind that? Does that get you excited without completely intimidating you? Great! Go for it!

More steps supporting your dream
It's easy to look at our genealogy chart and imagine our ancestors doing all these cool, adventurous things ... like traveling West in a Conestoga wagon, sailing in an ancient three-masted schooner from Ireland to the New World, living in colorful places like Constantinople, Morocco or Siam. But the adventure gene didn't die with your forefathers and mothers. It's still alive and well in you.

Here's a quick list of things to keep in mind as you dream the next steps in your life. Who knows, the following may well be exactly what got your ancestors on their way as well.

- Choose a dream that excites you.
- The adventure has to be a stretch.
- Say "YES!" to this dream not just because it's more attractive than your current reality, say "YES!" because you really love it.
- Keep quiet about your dream. Be wise and don't share it with naysayers.
- Simultaneously keep watch for the opportunity makers that can help facilitate your dream.
- Start investing in your dream today!
- Build your dream step-by-step, letting triggers of happiness flood your awareness every time you contribute to it.
- Create future memories of your dream. In other words, imagine it so vividly that you can feel the feeling of having it and living it.
- Let go of the "how" but take every opportunity that shows up to make it happen
- Invest a lot of love into this dream. Don't doubt it. Nurture it.
- Do what it takes to make it happen—even if some of the short-term steps aren't fun. (Like starting to exercise to lose weight and feel better. Most likely those first few days at the gym won't be fun. Just focus on the fact that you're taking steps to accomplish your goal, and get excited about what you're doing. Lean into higher emotions.)
- Don't wander off course.
- Don't let your resources leak. If you have a goal that requires a certain amount of money—like buying a house—don't squander it on little things. Stick with the major goal.

- Make a point of being grateful for every step, no matter how small it is.
- Thank the adventure and thank those adventurous ancestors of yours!
- Acknowledge the growth this dream is bringing.
- After you've manifested your dream CELEBRATE!!
- I'm serious. CELEBRATE yourself.
- When you get an inner prompting, start looking for the next BIGGER adventure!

The above steps are how you teach your brain and your inner self to evolve and grow. And the great thing is, you're not just doing this for yourself. The more you choose MORE ... the more you say "Yes!" and go for your dreams, the more firmly you are laying the emotional DNA foundations for adventure, dreams, and satisfaction for future generations to come. And isn't that an amazing gift to pass down to your descendants?

Life is about evolution
It's the nature of life itself to grow and change. Similarly, it is the nature of family systems to grow and change. And the way they grow and change is through you and me!

It doesn't matter how stuck you or your family seem to be in a particular pattern. If you feel called to do things differently and break out of a rut, then YOU are being called to be the family change agent. Remember the man who came to me because he was terrified that he'd lose one of his legs by the time he was 55-years old? Talk about the power of belief and the power of emotions and being in the grip of an ancestral pattern! When he finally "got" that he was dealing with a pattern and not "fate" itself, and that his belief and his fear were attracting the very thing he didn't want to experience, he consciously chose to let go the fear. After that he was a free man. With two legs!

If he could change a chilling, seven-generations-long pattern like that, what can you change? What magic can you bring into your family system?

Breaking the chains of the past
It's time and then some for humanity to break the chains of the past and release dysfunctional thoughts, emotions and actions that keep us endlessly cycling through old patterns of pain, conflict, suffering—and yes, war.

The world can't help but become a better place when our best selves show up. Thing is, our best selves can't show up dragging a lot of physical, mental and emotional baggage from the past along with us.

The beauty of doing this work is, not only do you benefit from growth and positive change, but think of the pain and suffering you're sparing your descendants—the children and grandchildren who come after you who will have to try and disentangle limiting ancestral patterns because you didn't. Think of the cost to the world.

And then there's the not-so-small fact that as you grow and evolve there is a ripple effect. Emotions are contagious. I'm sure you've had the experience of being in a great mood and then you walk into a meeting or a party and start talking to people, and before you know it you're angry and upset for no apparent reason.

You might not have noticed because they had a smile plastered on their face, but you obviously met a "buzzkill"—somebody whose lower-frequency, unhappy emotions affect and drag down everyone around them. Fortunately, the exact opposite is also true. Studies show that a person emitting the vibes of contentment and love emit a heart rate variability coherence state that positively affects the emotions of people around them up to 15 feet away![12] Which adds a whole new meaning to being the life of a party.

It is quite true that we lift each other up. Which means when you do positive work like Genealogy 3.0, you are helping not only yourself, your family and your immediate relationships, you actually begin to spread joy and positivity—higher emotions that cascade into the big world out there, making it a better place for all.

Imagine ... all this happening because you decided to get your genealogy chart done, and then wondered where else that information could take you!

Thank you

Thank you for joining me on this genealogical self-discovery journey. I hope you have found the information valuable and continue to apply the tools as you move through your life

There are more resources available on my website: www.judywilkins-smith.com. And if you want to get a more thorough grounding in Systemic Work & Constellations, check out my book *Decoding Your Emotional Blueprint: A Powerful Guide to Transformation Through Disentangling Multigenerational Patterns*. It's available on Amazon and through all major bookstores.

I also hold several transformational events during the course of the year on such topics as Money DNA (yes, we pass down money patterns!) Emotional DNA, Relationship DNA and Leadership DNA. It would be lovely to see you there!

ENDNOTES

1   "The long-term effects of extreme war-related trauma on the second generation of Holocaust survivors," Violence Vict 2009;24(5):687-700

2   "Parental advisory: maternal and paternal stress can impact offspring neurodevelopment,"
Biol Psychiatry. 2018 May 15; 83(10): 886–894.

3   "Intergenerational Transfer of Epigenetic Information in Sperm," Cold Spring Harb Perspect Med. 2016 May; 6(5

4   "Epigenetic Influence of Stress and the Social Environment," ILAR Journ, 2012, Dec; 53(3-4): 279-288.

5   "Intergenerational transmission of trauma--empirical research and family dynamics approach,"
Prax Kinderpsychol Kinderpsychiatr. 2012;61(8):564-83.

6   https://www.ncbi.nlm.nih.gov/pmc/articles/PMC¬¬2947916/

7   https://bscb.org/learning-resources/softcell-e-learning/epigenetics-its-not-just-genes-that-make-us/

8   https://www.nytimes.com/2018/01/31/science/dutch-famine-genes.html

9   BMJ 2021;374:n203, "COVID-19: Children born during the pandemic score lower on cognitive tests, study finds"

10   https://www.medrxiv.org/content/10.1101/2021.08.10.21261846v1.full.pdf

11   Prevalence and Associated Factors of Emotional and Behavioural Difficulties during COVID-19 Pandemic in Children with Neurodevelopmental Disorders (Children (Basel). 2020 Sep 4;7(9):128.); Covid-19: Children born during the pandemic score lower on cognitive tests, study finds (BMJ 2021;374:n2031)

12   Face masks reduce emotion-recognition accuracy and perceived closeness (PLoS One. 2021 Apr 23;16(4):e0249792.)

www.ingramcontent.com/pod-product-compliance
Ingram Content Group UK Ltd.
Pitfield, Milton Keynes, MK11 3LW, UK
UKHW020708090625

6297UKWH00046B/1082